A RADICAL APPROACH TO CONSERVATIVE INVESTING

by Kenneth S. Hogg

A RADICAL APPROACH TO CONSERVATIVE INVESTING

by Kenneth S. Hogg

"This book is published by The Episcopal Diocese of Northern Michigan in gratitude for the life and ministry of Ken and Mildred Hogg."

Thanks to Dan Weingarten along with Tom and Peg Lippart who spent considerable time reshaping tables and editing.

Copyright 2001
The Episcopal Diocese of Northern Michigan
131 E. Ridge Street, Marquette, MI 49855

Cover Designed by Ms. Erin Elizabeth Hogg

ISBN 0-9714242-0-9

TABLE OF CONTENTS

FOREWORD

One might wonder why a diocese of The Episcopal Church would want to publish this book. The answer takes us back to September of 1993. In that year I had been bishop of the Episcopal Diocese of Northern Michigan for eleven years and as bishop, I was also president of The Trust Association of the diocese overseeing all invested assets. In that month Mildred Hogg, the wife of the author, urged me once again to read Ken's book. I patiently or impatiently agreed that I would. It took some searching to find the manuscript she had given me months earlier. Finding it I brought it home to be read on evenings I could not sleep.

As I scanned and then read this book I was amazed. I read. Went to bed. Restlessly got up and read more. Frequently that night I laid down only to return again and again to the text. I was reading concepts that I already knew, but never had these truths been so clearly articulated for me. The content was so transforming for me that I immediately did two things.

I had a copy of Ken's manuscript sent to every member of The Trust Association of the diocese and I took Ken a copy of our portfolios and asked for his critique of those funds supporting the program and budget of the diocese. I pointed out to Ken, as I delivered to him a print-out of our investments, that we had proudly doubled our net asset value in the last 15 years.

On the 16th of November 1993 I received a four page single spaced letter. Among many observations and recommendations, Ken wrote, "I'm sure you won't be surprised that I have concluded the Diocesan funds are in trouble." I was not surprised, I was shocked. Ken went on to say, "My conclusion is based on three things: the composition of the investments, the shrinking of their value, and the haphazard management of the common stocks.... During the past 15 years the average annual inflation has been 5.7%. While the dollar value of the funds has doubled, the dollar itself has lost 59% of its value and is now worth $.41. The funds therefore, have lost 18% of their value, their purchasing power. I predict that with the present structure they will lose half their remaining value in six years."

Ken outlined how our investments might have done were they invested following his principles The contrast was sobering. Then he observed, "This is a drastic change, and certainly can't be done without a lot of advance education and persuasion. A lot of attitudes must be changed, possibly including your own. It also will require a whole new outlook and philosophy in your team. They would have to understand and freely acknowledge that the present course is nothing short of a disaster. Since they were the navigators, this will not be easy. You may need to clean house."

As members of The Trust Association we intended to be responsible, and we believed those advising us to be responsible. Yet we were headed in a direction that in time would have jeopardized the financial security of our diocese.

Fortunately the members of The Trust Association did not become defensive. We read Ken's letter and the book he had written, <u>A Radical Approach to Conservative Investing</u>. We adapted his strategy and for the first time took responsibility for our own investment policy and decisions. Beginning in January of 1994 we started reconfiguring our investments. After the first three full years under Ken's principles we had experienced extraordinary results.

In the three years between 1995 and 1997 our net worth doubled and that is after subtracting capital additions and all the income withdrawn for the support of our diocesan budget during those three years. True, these first three years were good years in the stock market. But we were prepared to take advantage of them and we are now in a much more secure position to weather any lean years.

With Ken's book and a subscription to Value Line we developed a clear and simple criteria with which we could follow a select number of stocks—a strategy that reasonable adults could follow with a reasonable time commitment. We own about two dozen very select stocks and we examine them quarterly. As long as they conform to our clear and simple standards we keep them indefinitely. When they no longer conform, we sell them. We do not try to be clever or smart in timing the market. In the past we had a "balanced portfolio" which was relentlessly eroded by inflation and we often took capital gains in the performing stocks while keeping the underperforming. As one member said, "Tom, it's scary when I think back on how we made decisions ten years ago."

This book you hold in your hands has brought The Diocese of Northern Michigan to a financial security of which we had only dreamed. Many of us on the trust have shared the unpublished manuscript of this book with numerous friends and family. All of us and the other various institutions we serve have been significantly influenced by this book and financially advantaged. Ken's financial savvy and Mildred's loyal support have been a gift to many. We are convinced that having read this book, you will join the grateful many. Ken died in the year 2000. Our regret is that we did not publish this book in time to have him see it in print and sign personal copies for us.

Thomas K. Ray,
Retired Bishop of Northern Michigan

PREFACE

Are You Dissatisfied with the Performance of Your Investments?

Of course you are, or you would not be reading this book. Before we can start talking about a cure, I must remind you of a rather uncomfortable proverb: "If you want something done right, do it yourself." You can think of a dozen reasons why it would be inconvenient, or impractical, or impossible for you to assume active management of your investments, but I have another proverb: "The fox knows many things, but the porcupine knows one **BIG** thing." Like the porcupine, I know one big thing - If you are lazy, unaware, and satisfied with results a little south of mediocre, mutual funds and full service brokers will suit you very well. But if excellence is important to you and if you want a more secure and comfortable retirement, you had better do it yourself.

On the surface it may seem strange that an investor with limited experience could outperform an experienced "expert". It is true, however, and the reasons will become obvious as we go along.

This book is not a magic wand. If your investments are successful, it will be your doing. My job is to show you the way and to help you develop the self-confidence you will need to make your investment decisions. The responsibility for your future welfare is yours. You can relinquish this task to a hired hand, a broker, mutual fund manager, or the like. But if you do, you can expect mediocre investment results. The problems of relying on investment professionals will be examined at some length later. Don't assume that your investment duties will be too complex or difficult. The burden is light, especially when you consider the benefits.

In this book you will find ideas and strategies that are unconventional and even radical from the perspective of the investment professional. This suggests a natural question. "How come this guy, that no one ever heard of, claims to know more than all these trained and highly paid experts?" Well, I do have several qualifications. First, I have been a successful investor for 67 years, longer than any of these experts have lived. Second, in the past 24 years in retirement my assets have increased more than 5 fold. Third, instead of making a living advising others how to invest, my income depends on my skill at investing my own money. In any case, the experts have not done too well for you lately. Maybe it is a point in my favor that I am not one of them. At this point you do not know whether my medicine will work, but at least it is not a sure loser. After reading the book, you still do not have to adopt my ideas but I think you will and, if you do, I am sure you will be glad you did.

P.S.

It has occurred to me that there may be some readers who are perfectly satisfied with their investments. This will never do. If you are reading purely for entertainment, I will soon have an ex-reader and that will be bad for both of us. It will hurt my pride and your pocketbook. It is against my principles, but I hope to change the mind of such a reader.

Just Like the Movies

Like the movies and TV, I will give you a teaser, an advance peek at coming attractions. You will be SO overwhelmed with curiosity, envy, and GREED that you'll want to come in the tent and see the whole show - and get in on the hot action.

A Tale of Two Portfolios

The first one is typical of an average investor, perhaps something like yours, the date 11/30/86.

TABLE 1

This is a very respectable portfolio. The stocks marked with an asterisk are among the 15 most popular stocks. All are well established, highly respected companies that offer high quality goods or services. Twenty percent of the assets are invested in bonds, about half that recommended by leading brokerage firms. This deviation is to improve growth. Following is a summary of the result after 10 years:

COMPANY	Number of SHARES	Price/Share	Annual Income	Total Value
AT&T *	400	25	480	10,000
DuPONT	111	90	340	9,990
EXON	152	66	547	10,032
GEN'L ELEC *	132	76	312	10,032
GEN'L MOTORS *	139	72	348	10,008
IBM *	80	125	625	10,000
PACIFIC G&E *	416	24	790	9,984
SEARS *	233	43	410	10,019
TREASURY BONDS	20	1,000	1,400	20,000
TOTALS			5,252	100,065

TABLE 1A

Average portfolio - 11/29/96

COMPANY	Number of SHARES	Price/Share	Annual Income	Total Value	RETURN
AT&T *	400	39	528	15,600	8.0
DuPONT	333	94	759	31,302	14.5
EXON	304	94	961	28,576	14.4
GEN'L ELEC *	528	104	972	54,912	20.6
GEN'L MOTORS *	278	58	445	16,124	7.9
IBM *	80	159	223	12,720	3.3
PACIFIC G&E *	416	24	495	9,984	5
SEARS *	233	50	214	11,650	3.6
TREASURY BONDS	20,000	1	1,400	20,000	7
TOTALS			5,997	200,862	

Although income has not increased substantially, asset value has more than doubled. While performance is hardly sparkling, average investors would probably feel comfortable with this result. That is, unless they took a closer look at where the profit was being generated. They might notice that 30% of their assets were doing most of the work and GE especially stands out. They might wonder if there were more companies like GE. It might help to have more workers and fewer innocent bystanders.

A Working Portfolio

Most investors want their savings to work hard for them and get very good results. It can be done, and it is not too difficult, but very few know how to do it. In the following portfolio, I used different criteria in selecting the companies and the result, too, is very different.

TABLE 2
Portfolio Selected for Growth and Safety - 11/30/86

COMPANY	Number of SHARES	Price/Share	Annual Income	Total Value
Albertson	217	46	191	9,982
American Int't Group	81	124	36	9,990
Auto Data Processing	357	28	114	9,996
Campbell Soup	167	60	220	10,020
General Electric	132	76	312	10,032
McDonald's	167	60	110	10,020
Merck	96	104	181	9,984
Servicemaster	476	21	402	9,996
Walgreen	313	32	163	9,984
TOTALS			1,991	100,020

TABLE 2A
Portfolio Selected for Growth and Safety - 11/29/96

COMPANY	Number of SHARES	Price/Share	Annual Income	Total Value	RETURN
Albertson	1736	35	1042	60,760	21.5
American Int't Group	456	115	182	52,440	18.3
Auto Data Processing	1428	43	657	61,404	21
Campbell Soup	668	83	1029	55,444	20.6
General Electric	528	104	972	54,912	20.6
McDonald's	1002	47	301	47,094	17.4
Merck	864	83	1,382	71,712	23.7
Servicemaster	1607	26	1,093	41,782	18.1
Walgreen	1252	42	601	52,584	19.2
Wrigley	1248	58	849	72,384	23.8
TOTALS			8,078	570,516	

The Tip of the Iceberg

It is no more work to invest in excellent stocks than in mediocre, but clearly the exercise is well worth while. The 10-year difference is enough to interest any investor, but over a 30 year period the magic of compounding would make the difference more than 20 fold instead of almost triple. Stock selection and compounding, among many other things will be covered in detail later.

INTRODUCTION

Investing, an American Tradition

What is the average citizen to think about investing? We all know that saving is a cardinal virtue, and that the investing of these savings builds the factories and creates the jobs that make our country strong and prosperous, and such investments create profits for the investor. As members of this society we all have the opportunity to participate in this activity and share in the benefits. Despite these advantages millions of our citizens avoid these transactions either from fear of risking their savings, thinking they know too little to be successful, or perhaps thinking this occupation is only the province of the rich. These misconceptions will be dealt with later in the hope that it will encourage more people to become investors.

Still, It is Not for Everyone

Having described the universal values of investing, I must also admit there are some exceptions. To profit from the method of investing I will describe, a person needs several attributes, which most of us have. First, one should have enough interest in the venture to give it some time and attention. To get the best results, one should take complete charge of one's finances. If electing to pay an advisor, the investor should still participate in the decision making. Second, the investor should treat his or her investment program as a business, not a hobby. Decisions are not made off hand or on impulse. They are carefully considered and are made for logical business reasons. Third, and for many the most difficult quality, one needs an even temperament. While the stock market is very stable and predictable over the long run, it is subject to considerable short-term volatility. Short-term traders are like a flock of sparrows. They may be settled peacefully, but at the slightest excuse they all take off together in one direction or another and before long they are back where they started. If you have bought shares in a good solid company that continues to have good earnings and sales, these gyrations do not affect the long-term value of the stock. It is difficult at first to ignore a sharp drop, but panic selling is the surest way to lose money.

If you are unable to manage these three qualifications, and especially the third one, you are better off with CDs, Savings bonds, or the Money Market. These are not, in my view profitable investments and you may lose money through inflation, but it will not be as fast.

Is Investing Safe?

Practically speaking, the best place to invest is the stock market. What kind of risk does this entail? From the media stories you might think it a frantic and dangerous place. People make and lose fortunes, sometimes in a few minutes. For some, the very danger is attractive, but many potential investors would just as soon swim in the shark tank as risk their hard-earned savings in such an uncertain and frightening arena. So most of us avoid it. The truth is that investing is like a power tool. A table saw with a knowledgeable and careful operator is a productive and accurate machine. In careless or unskilled hands it can inflict terrible injuries. If you use reasonable, common sense precautions, investing in stocks is safe and profitable.

Dr. Jekyll or Mr. Hyde?

The popular image of the stock market is misleading. The things we hear may be true. This is the stock market's dark side, it's "Mr. Hyde" mode. But there is also "Dr. Jekyll". There are what amounts to two entirely different institutions living in the same body. The difference in the two modes is caused, not so much by any institutional difference as by the attitudes of the investors. Just as a hammer can build or destroy, the same facilities of the stock exchange that serve a serious long term investor are just as convenient for the investor who speculates. Speculators are far from a homogeneous group. Some are big time operators who often perform a useful service in financing new industries, among other things, and some are the feather merchants, people of modest means who are in it for thrills, adventure, and entertainment, a substitute for roulette or black jack. Their activities, whether constructive or frivolous, have no effect on our decisions. Speculators represent the Mr. Hyde investing mode and their follies or problems should not discourage us from participating in profitable activity. The Dr. Jekyll mode is a calm, sober place of business no more dangerous or confusing than your neighborhood supermarket. With the kind of guidance this book provides, the average person can invest with safety, confidence, and profit.

How to Get Started

Before we start the actual instruction, a brief outline of my investment strategy is timely. At the start I should say that my ideas as well as my methods are unconventional and in substantial conflict with traditional ideas. This is not accidental. Being naturally of a conservative disposition, I respect and value tradition and custom. Much of what is old and familiar can be retained without doing violence to real progress. However, there are times when the dead hand of tradition can't be permitted to interfere with progress, much less profit. An example of this is the persistence of the theory among investment professionals that bonds are a conservative investment. Despite all evidence and experience to the contrary this doctrine persists. A lot will be said about this later, but the situation reinforces the warning of Admiral Grace Hopper, a brilliant computer pioneer, who said that it is smart to remember that it has been said that the most dangerous words in the English language are, "We've <u>always</u> done it that way." When tradition parts with logic and common sense, I part with tradition. I have tried my best to build my investment philosophy on logic and have rigorously excluded any exceptions.

What is our Purpose?

To build an investment program that would be the most beneficial to average investors I have had to make certain assumptions as to their objectives. These have been strongly influenced by my own experiences. Here is what I believe the investor wants:

1. A long term commitment with a long-range purpose such as building a fund for children's education or a nest egg for protection during retirement years.

2. The most efficient investment of savings, the maximum accumulation of assets while considering, and balancing two factors, a high return, and protection against loss, a safe investment.

> a. The return on an investment is made up of two figures, the first is the yield, or the amount paid out each year in dividends or interest, and the second is "appreciation" the growth in value of the investment. No matter how good a company is otherwise, unless its earnings grow steadily and strongly, it is not much use as a long-term investment.

> b. Safety is as important as earnings. Profits are not much consolation if a company fails. To protect against this possibility we consider a company's financial strength. Before buying, we examine its past performance, and even then we do not put all our eggs in one basket. We spread our investment over ten or twelve companies in various industries.

3. A program not too technical or difficult to understand; it must be straightforward and logical - something a person of normal intelligence can understand and in which he or she can have confidence.

4. Something not too time consuming or otherwise burdensome. This does not mean that investors can take the activity lightly. This is a very important project. Their children's success in life and their own future comfort and security may depend on how they do the job. It will require regular and serious attention, but not so much time and energy as to interfere with work or family life.

In my program I have tried to balance these factors in a reasonable way, but in the end it will be your own application of the program that will make it work.

What about Other Investment Strategies?

Would it improve your investment skills to read as many other books on the subject as possible? In many circumstances, the more information, the better, but if there is a great deal of information, much of it contradictory, the result could be confusing. There are always many different possible routes to go from the Post Office to the fairgrounds, but, if you don't know the way, it is less confusing to be given one route rather than several alternatives. To show what I mean, I will quote from two different books about investments, written by well-known professionals.

Example #1

The following is from a book by a well-known former fund manager, one of the most successful:

"There are all kinds of complicated formulas for figuring out what percentage of your assets should be put into stocks, but I have a simple one, and it is the same for Wall Street as it is for the racetrack. Only invest what you can afford to lose ..."

To a non-investor, especially one that already thinks of the stock market as a more respectable Las Vegas, this advice has the ring of common sense. But consider the source. This author was entrusted with the investment of literally billions of dollars, much of it the life savings of people of modest means. Could his investors afford to lose their earnings? Absolutely NOT! And yet he invested these precious assets in (horrors) stocks. Did these investors lose their savings? No indeed, after paying management fees and expenses, they had modest profits. These were not risky investments. As the author knew, better than anyone else, carefully selected common stocks are the safest and most profitable investments. That 'one liner' about the racetrack is quotable and it may be a real zinger for selling his book, but it is very poor investment advice.

Example #2

Another very prominent author has published the following:

"Common stock is just like merchandise that is bought and sold for a profit. You, as the merchant, must sell your merchandise in order to realize a profit."

Again a person lacking experience could easily mistake this for sensible advice. It is, of course, possible to treat stocks this way, as if they were just coupons or lottery tickets, but they are in reality something very different. Each share of stock represents ownership of a small part of a large company. The important money is made by owning stock and holding on to it in a profitable company.

Buy and Hold

As I sit here today, I am looking at the record of a stock purchase I made 15¾ years ago. It cost me $29,404, today it is worth $257,000 and pays $6,160 in dividends this year, a yield of 21% on the original cost, and that increases about 10% each year. Extraordinary? Not at all. American Home Products is a very good company, or I wouldn't own it, but it is the slowest growing in my portfolio. The only thing that is unusual is that anyone holds a stock for 15 years. The smartest, and eventually the richest, investor is the one who can pick stocks whose profitability continues indefinitely and who never sells them. Consider the purchase I used as an example. The cost included a commission of $154, but since then I have paid nothing and the only paper work required has been to endorse the dividend checks. I expect to keep it the rest of my life, which may be another 15 years. It may not grow that fast in the future, but if it should, it will be worth $1.8 million with an annual dividend of about $45,000. In a later chapter I'll discuss what to do if a stock's performance is unsatisfactory.

Missed Opportunity(?)

Fifteen years ago these books had not been written and I did not have the benefit of the wise counsel they offer. Had I followed the advice in example 1, I would have bought a CD and I would still have $29,000. Had I followed example 2, I would have had a busy 15 years trading stocks. Since traders are as apt to lose as to win, I might have lost it all. If successful, I would have made hundreds of trades, paid hundreds of commissions, generated hundreds of capital gains taxes and, even with all that work, it is very unlikely I would have done as well.

What about the Rich and Famous?

In 1995 Jack Kemp, through his broker Merrill Lynch, did a lot of trading, a total of 189 trades. After trading $2 million in securities, he wound up with a loss of $77,000. I do not know how much he started with, but surely more than his loss, and, in 1995, $77,000 invested in the S&P 500 stocks would have resulted in a gain of $27,000. Consider this and learn the easy way instead of the hard way.

Be Skeptical

Be skeptical of all investment advice regardless of the source, including mine. Test it with evidence and your own common sense. Unless it passes your tests with flying colors, reject it because there is a lot more bad advice around than good. The snappy one liners in examples 1 & 2 may help sell books, but they are lousy investment advice.

How is This Book Different?

I will list below the features that I believe make this book unique:

1. To me, the most important innovation is expanding the role, and the responsibility of the investors in the management of their own assets. The independence and self-reliance of the person who, after all, is most affected by the quality of this management is the keystone of the whole program I have developed. This affects every aspect of successful investing and you will hear a lot about it as we go along.

2. The investors must also understand that the handling of their savings is a serious and important business. It is not a hobby or something to look at when they have the time. It should be run like a business with careful selection of stocks and a regular review of those currently held.

3. To make self-management possible and to facilitate businesslike operation, the process of selection and review of stocks has been streamlined so they can be clearly understood and not be too burdensome.

4. I mentioned it earlier but this book also offers guidance and steers investors toward a particular type of investment. To some this may seem to go too far, but I believe my readers need and want guidance, and I have a responsibility to them. People who don't need advice won't buy or read this book.

5. While this feature is included in the others, I want to place special emphasis on minimizing the expense of investment services. In my opinion, these services, investment advice and asset management are wildly overpriced and their quality ranges from mediocre to poor. While there are certainly brokers, advisers, and asset managers who are individually competent, they are hampered by the whole structure of the business with its unavoidable reliance on mass production. If investors will take charge of their assets, they can save a lot of money and, at the same time, achieve a better result.

Complexity

In the evaluation of stocks it is traditional to process a mass of data that would choke a horse. Each company has hundreds of characteristics that can be studied. Some of these items are of critical importance, like financial status, earnings growth, revenue growth, price compared to earnings. Some are negligible. There are other measurements that would be very important in rating companies that are shaky to start with, but they do not concern us because we would not be buying any of those. If a company passes the tests of the criteria we select, the considerable added investigation sometimes recommended is unlikely to prove worthwhile.

There is another advantage to keeping the list of criteria short. Especially when starting out a mass of data creates confusion and it is difficult to keep everything in perspective. It is not unlikely that an investor will fix on some particular item and give it greater weight than it deserves.

The Pot of Gold

It is well known that, if a thing seems too good to be true, it probably is. But the idea of instant riches, of making a killing in the market is an attractive dream, and there are many promoters who are trying to make that dream come true - for themselves at your expense.

The End of the Rainbow

If a book's dust cover tells of a sure way to make a million in the market, or a salesman offers you a security that will triple in value in a month or two, why give you the secret? When you have a good thing going you should keep it quiet. Bessie Smith found this out the hard way, as she related in a sad song:

> When you get good lovin'
> Never go and spread the news.
> Gals will double-cross you, and
> Leave you with the Empty Bed Blues.

Is it possible that these promoters have a different secret? Could it be more profitable to sell treasure maps than to dig for treasure? These entrepreneurs may be spiritual descendants of an old Hindu who had clever fingers and often astonished observers by changing a piece of lead into gold. He placed a lump of lead on a table and covered it with a cloth. After passing his hand over it and mumbling a magic word, he whipped off the cloth and there was a lump of gold.

The Fatal Warning

This feat was greatly admired and many people wanted to learn how to do it. The old man was perfectly willing to share the secret but, since it was the key to untold wealth he was entitled to a generous fee. After giving the instructions and disclosing the magic word, he was careful to warn his pupils of one danger. If when attempting this transmutation anyone were to think of brown monkeys, it wouldn't work. Unfortunately none of his pupils was ever able to purge his mind of the brown monkeys. Maybe the Hindu and his modern disciples are selling the wrong secret.

Who's the Goat?

As I thought about this phantom treasure, I suddenly remembered a story my father told me many years ago. When he was a small boy in Brooklyn, there was a lot of vacant land inhabited by large numbers of goats that had run wild. He desperately wanted one for a pet. An older boy, an expert, told him how to catch one. All he had to do was to put salt on its tail. It would immediately become tame and docile. After a few hours stalking the goats with a salt shaker, my father finally understood that he was the goat.

What About My Own Qualifications?

The first point in my favor is that I am not an Investment Professional, a member of the fraternity that lives by furnishing advice and services to investors. I am a professional investor. Success in investing keeps meat on my table and will provide security and comfort in my old age. I do not collect a fee up front for every transaction, so, like you, I take a loss very seriously.

Secondly, I have been successful. I have been retired for 23 years. Investments are the main source of my earnings and my income is 5 or 6 times my salary the last year I worked.

Third, I am very old and very wise. At my age a person is either very wise or very foolish. I have turned out wise - I think, although I often wonder why I am beating my brains out writing this book. As an investor I have seen everything, the Depression, the crash of '87, three major wars, serving in two of them, and this colossal Bull Market.

And last, while not cautious or timid, I am the world's most conservative investor, aiming for maximum return with minimum risk.

A Family Tradition

Another factor in my favor is a family tradition of investing that goes back almost 150 years. From my earliest childhood I was aware that investing was an important ingredient in our family life. My grandfather, an immigrant from Scotland, was investing in stocks shortly after the Civil War. My father, still in his teens, was investing before the turn of the century. His brother and sisters followed the same pattern. Like good Scots, they were all conservative long-term investors. They invested in solid, profitable companies - no speculation or trading, or buying on margin. And, unlike many less prudent investors, survived the Depression unscathed. These examples have served me well during my 67 years as an investor.

The Graveyard Shift

In July of 1929, when I was 18 and had just completed my freshman year of college, I had a summer job on the graveyard shift at an oil refinery in Bayway, New Jersey. In that month I got my start as an investor by putting part of my pay into stock. I was the eldest sibling, and my sister and brothers followed the family tradition in turn. Now my children and grandchildren, have become the fourth and fifth generations of investors. All have been careful and conservative investors and all have prospered.

Retirement. A new Beginning

After 40 years of work and 44 of investing, I retired - from my employment, but not from business. I still work for a living, deriving most of my earnings from investments. In my 23 years in retirement I have not only improved my investment skills, but I can better appreciate the vital importance of the savings I accumulated before retirement. They have played a major role in making my retirement secure and comfortable.

Investor Oriented

My investment philosophy has been forged by my background and many years of experience and has been strongly influenced by my solutions to the difficult transition from employment to retirement. For many readers retirement will seem a long way off, but it is the target and, unless you set your sights on it now, you may miss the mark.

What? No Volunteers?

There may well be others who from long experience may be better qualified to write this book, but I do not see any of them stepping up to the plate. I am in the position of the young Air Force Lieutenant who was teaching a class in Photo Intelligence. There were quite a few senior officers in the class, and the Lieutenant started off by saying, "There are many people in the Air Force who know more about this subject than I do." He paused and looked carefully around the room. "But I do not see any of them here." So he went ahead with the class.

A Tough Book for a Tough Job

Do not think I have a magic formula that will make it easy to achieve your objectives. There is a lot of meat in this book, and it is not all tender. To digest it properly takes a lot of chewing. Look at it this way; you can skim through it, and you may get a C or a C+. But you are not just working for a piece of paper or a certificate of attendance this time. You are grown up now. This is real life. If you get an A, you'll have a safer and more pleasurable retirement, and that could easily last 30 years, a third of your whole lifetime. The first, essential step, saving, is the hardest, especially getting started, but it gets easier as you go along. The next step is investing the savings. This requires advance study and careful attention, but it produces a great sense of accomplishment and satisfaction as you see your savings grow. The next step is having it when it starts to support you when you need it. Finally, if it is important to you, the residue can be of great help to your children or grandchildren.

This book is tough. I do not mince words or compromise on principle. I do my best to tell it like it is.

Expensive Baggage

There will be a lot more discussion of it later, but it is my view that investment services are priced too high, much too high, and can eat up a large percentage of your potential profit. What is worse, although there are exceptions, most of them provide no benefit whatever to the investor. But times are changing - very slowly. There are opposing trends. One toward simpler and less expensive services, such as discount brokers, which is moving with the speed of a glacier. The opposite trend toward more expensive and more useless services is going more like an express train.

Although there is still a very long way to go, and we are still going in the wrong direction, some investors are becoming more savvy and are learning to avoid some of the expense that we used to take for granted. This is not the place for a detailed treatment of the subject, but it is not too soon to alert you to the problem. At every step you should think about costs and how to minimize them.

The Lord Helps those who Help Themselves

I must say, however, that critical as I am of investment professionals in general, the fault is not entirely, or even principally theirs. It is a law of nature that when pigeons walk around waving money, it attracts the hawks. While I do not admire the predators, it is hard to feel sorry for investors who have more money than brains. But there are many people who are prudent and don't want to be exploited, and that is what this book is about.

Will the Real Stock Market Please Stand Up?

The stock market is like Times Square. It can look very different, depending on your objective. If you stand at Broadway and 42nd Street and want to go to 59th Street, Broadway is just a direct route to your destination. If, on the other hand, you want entertainment, you can sample the diversions offered by Times Square, the adult movies, the massage parlors, the peep shows, the bars, restaurants, street musicians, or 3 card Monte on the sidewalk. It may be fun, but it does not get you anywhere. This book takes the direct route, skipping the sideshows.

The Book

One of the most important purposes of your savings and investment program is to build a retirement fund to supplement the shrinking "Entitlements" and company benefit plans. It is time to realize the honeymoon is over. As we struggle to get a handle on the deficit, we will begin to focus on reality. We can not live in Wonderland forever, where our comfortable life style will always be subsidized by Federal borrowing. This will not all happen at once. Public resistance and political timidity will slow the process. Nevertheless the squeeze has already begun and none of us will live to see it end. The time for you to start countermeasures is NOW.

Are you Hungry?

I hope you are, because I have talked to hundreds of investors and, unless they are dissatisfied or really determined to reach for excellence, they will not change. This is perfectly reasonable, if it ain't broke, don't fix it. Unless people want a change or are curious enough to look at alternatives, they will not get much benefit from this book.

Independence

A vital ingredient in successful investing is acceptance of the concept that the investors themselves are the only ones responsible for the success, or failure, of their investments. With no excuses or scapegoats to blame, the investors will focus on honing their own skills.

A Question of Balance

My challenge is to develop a safe and effective system of investing that will not be so burdensome or complicated that you, and other investors that would benefit, will reject it. There is a tremendous amount of information available, more than any human can digest, but, as I said earlier, these items of information are not all equal. For practical reasons we must establish priorities and draw a line. The priorities I will suggest are intended to insure that you will not lose sight of the important factors or devote a lot of time and attention to trivialities. This approach is unconventional, and that is exactly what is needed to strip away some of the obsolete conventions and myths that discourage self-management and drive investors to rely on professionals.

How can the Average person Learn to Pick Stocks?

I will describe a straightforward, common sense approach that anyone can apply successfully. In designing this method I recognized that you have a full time job, a family, and other interests and that time as well as money is valuable to you. There is no sense in offering you an investment process so sophisticated and time consuming that you will not want to use it. The assignment of priorities will ease the burden. By focusing on half a dozen of the most important, omitting the rest, we can, I believe, get about 95% of the useful information.

What about the Other 5%?

It would be impossible to do everything, so there must be a cut off somewhere. My judgment surely is not infallible, and no two people would agree on the same list. Professionals especially might criticize omissions for two reasons. First, complexity is meat and drink to them, and secondly it is not in their interest to encourage self-management of investment assets. Theoretically, it would be desirable to get closer to 100% of the useful information, but, at this point, the going gets tougher. To get one more percentage point, from 95% to 96% might double your time and effort, and I consider that impractical. Of course as time goes on you may want to get deeper into the subject and polish your skills. Do so, by all means, but in the meantime don't worry about it, just perfect your understanding of the most important factors.

Format of the Book

Although this method is businesslike and easy to apply, a successful investment program cannot depend on a list of rules alone. Objectives, standards and rules are necessary tools, but the market environment is changeable and unpredictable. There will be surprises, situations where the rules don't exactly fit. An investor must have the intelligence and flexibility to meet unusual situations while still observing his basic objectives. To make the best decisions in unforeseen circumstances he needs to understand some of the basic forces that will be affecting his portfolio. Some are not thoroughly understood by most people. For this reason, I have divided the book into two parts. The first concentrates on these basic forces such as inflation, risk, and compound earnings. This section is not long or burdensome, but it is an important part of an independent investor's background. I urge you to give it special attention.

Features of this Investment System

There are four features that I believe, in combination, distinguish this method from any others I know about.

> 1. The emphasis is that you should understand thoroughly the basic principles that affect investment results. The early chapters of this book are devoted to reviewing these principles.

> 2. This system reduces the items of information about a company that an investor needs to know, limiting these to a half dozen or so items that are easily found and easily understood. This avoids wasting time and energy sifting through a mass of information of slight or negligible value, and makes the system more acceptable to those who could benefit from it without omitting any vital factors.

> 3. Discipline. The adoption of strict investor selected standards or rules is intended to measure a stock's suitability as a long-term investment. These standards in practice act as a screening device, weeding out the unfit. To be successful these rules must be followed religiously.

> 4. Last, an integral and vital feature is the individual's acceptance and application of the principle of self-management.

These are the key elements of my investment system. **DO IT YOURSELF.**

I have done my best to provide a reliable method that the average person can use to invest safely and profitably for his or her retirement fund.

Do not Get Poor

Average people have a small chance of becoming really rich, but without careful planning, they have a good chance of becoming poor. This book is not a fairy tale. It is not about getting rich; it is about not getting poor.

CHAPTER 1

SAVING - STEP ONE

Number One is Retirement

There can be many reasons to save money, but from my perspective, having lived in retirement for many years, the most important one is for a fund to supplement your retirement income. Saving is always hard to do and easy to put off because it reduces current income that you would like to use right now. It is a sort of schizophrenia. Retirement seems so far in the future and you sort of resent this retired stranger who is making demands for money you need now. There will be plenty of time before retirement to see to his or her needs. But the day of reckoning is already on the track speeding toward you, and you had better be ready when it arrives. It will come sooner than you think, and it is urgent that you begin your preparation now - today. Every day counts and wasted time is greedily eating away at your future security. It will hurt you at the very time you are most vulnerable. There is hardly anything sadder than a frail elderly person, who has always lived comfortably, reduced to poverty and dependence on relatives or welfare, completely helpless. You can not imagine yourself in that position, but you better think about it now rather than 20 or 30 years from now. Inconvenient as it may be, we must accumulate our retirement fund during our working years, so the earlier we start the better. The whole focus of this book is on tailoring saving and investment plans and programs to make your retirement more comfortable and secure.

The Bad News

The good news is that you will live longer and retire earlier. The bad news is that, in a shorter working life, you must save enough to protect yourself during a longer period of retirement. Without careful planning and some sacrifice, you will probably outlive your money.

A Disturbing Trend

While many of the elderly get along quite well, there are more and more that do not. We read in the news and see on TV that there are large numbers of retirees that worked hard. They thought they were set for life, only to see their savings fall far short of their needs and expectations or even melt away completely, leaving them destitute. It does not seem fair to change the rules on pensions and taxes in the middle of the game, but, like it or not, we might as well realize that the number one rule is that rules can be changed without notice. And that is what has been happening and will surely continue. If anyone is still under the impression that it will all work out, it is time to wake up and face the facts. This is a problem for society as a whole, but for the individuals affected it is more like a disaster. Why is this happening, and how can we minimize the damage to ourselves?

Some of the Underlying Causes

1. There is chronic inflation. Although it has varied from about zero to perhaps 15%, over the past 70 years, it has averaged about 3.1%. There has been a long-term upward trend. It has moderated recently but for the next 10 or 15 years it is likely to average between 3 and 4%. This may not seem like a lot but, as we will see in a later chapter, its long-term effect can be devastating. This is especially true for those who have retired with fixed incomes, or who have invested their assets in bonds, CDs, the money market, or other securities that pay interest.

2. The intractable federal deficit aggravates all the other problems from inflation to taxes and entitlements.

3. Spiraling health care costs. Most Americans accept the proposition that all of our citizens, whatever their economic status, deserve access to health care. As I write there is no consensus as to how this can be accomplished, but few doubt that it will be expensive. The money must come from somewhere, and that means either increased taxes, reduction of other services, or most likely both. Either choice will affect retirees unfavorably.

4. Unsettled economic conditions and the relatively high cost of wages and benefits are putting pressure on business to cut expenses. This is likely to slow job formation and, of the jobs being created, more and more are part time, with few benefits or low pay or both.

5. Worst of all is the general reluctance of individuals to save and make adequate provision for future needs. For many people the closest they come to saving is to reduce their credit card debt occasionally. Most of us are amortizing our mortgages. When the mortgage is paid off we own our home free and clear and the big expense of monthly mortgage payments is eliminated. The regular mortgage payments may be the only savings program many people use, and it is very helpful to a retiree to be free of mortgage payments. Regrettably, however, banks and other lenders encourage homeowners to use the equities they have built up as collateral for loans, rather like second mortgages. This practice erodes our savings and jeopardizes our future security. The only bright side to this problem is that you do not have to fall into this trap.

Some Specific Problems

These unfavorable conditions cause some very specific difficulties. Some of these relate to pension plans, entitlements, and of course, taxes.

Pension Plans - Industrial

An Old Problem
In the past, pension plans usually had defined benefits related to pay level and length of service. There was always some uncertainty about these plans, since many companies did not set aside in advance the funds necessary to pay these pensions in case the company had financial problems. Even when the plans were ostensibly funded, companies were often over optimistic in their estimates of how these funds would grow. This practice would inflate the company's profits and create a corresponding deficit in the pension fund. Recent federal legislation establishes strict funding requirements for industrial, but not governmental pensions. This is fine for new plans, but some companies are in such a deep hole that it will be a long and difficult struggle before their pension funds are on a sound basis. For example, one of the country's largest employers recently had a multi-billion dollar deficit in its pension plan, which it is now making progress to correct.

A New Solution?
Now many companies, instead of promising definite retirement benefits, agree to a fixed <u>contribution to the retirement fund</u>.

Most of us now know how it works:

1. The company reaches an agreement with its union as to the general characteristic of the plan which will not be run by the company but by an outside fund manager. While this is the usual arrangement, sometimes the company manages the plan. This is a poor practice, since the company is more apt to mismanage the fund, especially to invest it in the company's own stock.

2. Since management of such a fund is a very profitable business, a swarm of insurance companies, banks, mutual funds, and brokers make proposals and the parties choose one as manager.

3. The manager will provide a selection of three or four ways the pension funds may be invested. Employees will be able to choose whether their portion of the fund will be invested in bonds, high growth stocks, income stocks or some mixture, depending on the offerings provided by the plan.

4. The plan manager will doubtless provide literature describing the choices and the company will probably furnish an adviser to assist employees make their choices. The selection of investments can have a dramatic effect on the final value of a pension. Unfortunately the literature is provided by the plan manager whose top priority is to increase the manager's own profit and it is very unlikely that the adviser will be well qualified.

5. On retirement the employees can usually elect to keep their accumulated assets invested in the plan and use the income as a pension or draw it out in a lump sum. The lump sum option is fraught with danger.

A Plus for the Employer

This kind of plan is very advantageous for the company. It knows the exact cost of the plan and it gets rid of responsibility. These plans put a burden of responsibility on the employee that few are well able to bear.

Free at Last

How will **ALL** these employees handle their new freedom? Now they feel a bit more in charge of their own destiny. But the ability of the average employee to make wise investment decisions, and especially to handle a lump sum payment that may amount to hundreds of thousands of dollars is doubtful, to say the least. While some will be successful, many will be like a two-year-old with a box of matches.

Investment Advice

The fund manager or some designated company employee provides investment advice, but, even in the unlikely event that the adviser is competent and unbiased, there is a problem. Without considerable background, the kind I am trying to furnish in this book, average employees cannot comprehend or digest the advice they really need. So, instead of advice tailored to their needs, the employees get a canned presentation that may well advise investing in a mixture of all available options. The adviser thus performs the classic CYA maneuver of keeping one foot on each base.

Lump Sum or Pension?

Suppose you have been carefully tracking the progress of your fund. Since it is very profitable for the fund manager, it is almost certainly lagging behind the S&P 500 Index. In other words even a mediocre investor could do better. This might suggest that you should take the Lump Sum option. The problem is that, if one suddenly receives a payment of half a million dollars or so, one might easily imagine oneself rich. Let us see what it really means. Since it will have to provide a supplemental income for 30 years or more, it must be safe; and the assets and income must outpace inflation. A half million invested as described would produce a monthly income of about $1,100, not a rich pension by any means, but both capital and income would increase at a rate of 6 to 8% per year, staying well ahead of inflation.

To achieve this result it would require iron self discipline to resist the temptation to spend any of the money and pretty good investment savvy, which you will have after digesting this book. But unless you have both of these ingredients, it might be better to skip the lump sum.

The Future of 401(k) Pensions

Their performance is mediocre. But that can probably be tolerated by the average employee. However I expect the lump sum option will cause very serious and wide-spread problems, but I do not see any way to unscramble that egg.

Pension Plans - Governmental

The Security of Governmental Pensions

You might think that public employees would be better protected than employees of private companies. Most are quite secure but there are a growing number of defaults in these plans. There is a fly in the ointment. It is no secret that lawmakers are reluctant to impose regulations on themselves or, perhaps as a matter of professional courtesy, on any governmental agency. Private companies are strictly controlled, with some loopholes for small business, to insure that their pension plans are financially sound. Government is presumed to be responsible and therefore is exempt from these regulations.

Nevertheless, it is shocking to see how public employees are sometimes treated in the matter of retirement benefits. The fact is that in some localities and in some whole states underfunding is so serious that benefits have been cut unilaterally and in a few cases the fund ran out completely and city finances have been placed under the control of a court.

The Bomb is Ticking

Until the money actually runs out, payments can be made as usual, although as the crisis approaches something has to be done. The difficulty is that a city or state that has under contributed for many years has dug itself in a very deep hole. To restore the plan to health it must first start paying what it should have been contributing all along. But a much greater problem is to make up for past under funding. All of this would require a massive tax increase or sharp cuts in benefits or both. There is no easy solution.

What to Do?

If you are a public employee, there are two things to do. First, start a saving and investment plan to supplement your pension or, if you already have such a plan, consider increasing the contributions. The second thing is to find out the status of your pension fund. If it is financially sound and fully funded, that is a good sign, but you still have to be alert, since it could be affected by future cost cutting programs. If financing is inadequate, do what you can, perhaps through your union, to resolve it.

Entitlements

In any serious effort to eliminate or even reduce the federal budget deficit, control of the "Entitlements", like Social Security, Medicare, Medicaid, and federal pensions, must be prime targets. While these areas are all politically sensitive, they involve federal expenditures that constitute such a large percentage of the budget that we will eventually have to do something about them. Whatever is done will certainly be hazardous to your wealth and will shift more of the burden of your support to your own shoulders.

Taxes

Even aside from the effects of a health care reform plan that aims toward universal coverage, taxes will certainly increase. The sad fact is we have not been paying our way. We still are not. We are using borrowed money to subsidize a life style we can not afford and it feels so good we do not want to stop. There will be continuous pressure for the foreseeable future to balance the budget, but not much enthusiasm for the necessary economies. There will surely be increased excise taxes on tobacco, alcohol, and luxury goods. There still may be broad-based energy or VAT taxes, or both, and other federal and local taxes can only go in one direction. Since the amount of increase and the specific targets are unknown, all we can do is beef up our retirement funds. This is a grim prospect, but being old, and sick, and also poor is grimmer yet.

A Rough Road

What this all comes down to is that we have a rough road ahead and it is uncertain at best what support we will get from others. This book offers no panacea, only guidance and encouragement. Nothing will be easy, but, on the other hand, nothing is impossible either. To cope with these problems we have to save smart and invest smart. As we will see, the first smart move to make is to start saving, preferably <u>yesterday</u>, but certainly no later than today.

CHAPTER 2

HORSEPOWER

Putting your Savings to Work

Saving is the first step, but it is only half the battle. You know that savings can be invested and will then start to work for you. What you also should appreciate is the tremendous difference it will make to your security and comfort in retirement, depending on HOW it is invested.

The Horse Trainer

Think of your money as a strong, willing horse. Your horse can work hard and productively, or it can just wander around the pasture grazing and romping happily in the sun. Your horse has no sense of direction, it does not know what it is supposed to do unless you train and supervise it. In the same way it is very easy for you to let your savings nibble gently at the low interest rates provided by a savings account, a CD, or a money fund. You will not have to strain your brain, you can forget about it. You can also forget about a comfortable and secure retirement. On the other hand you can apply your common sense and, with a little effort, make your savings really get to work.

Is Second Best OK?

You might think, well, it takes a lot of attention and effort to get the **best** results. I'm not that greedy, suppose the return from my investment is a couple of a percent less than I might get. That won't make much difference - will it? Let's see.

TABLE 3

Future Value of investing $200 a month for 30 years
Take Your Choice

Annual Return	Future Value
3%	116,839
5%	167,145
10%	455,865
12%	705,903
14%	1,111,411

This is a classroom exercise and it surely will not fit your own circumstances, but it accurately demonstrates the kind of nest egg you may accumulate and the big difference a couple of percentage points makes. Most of you will not have 30 years before retirement, but most will be able to save more than $50 a week and, if you increase it proportionately as your income increases, you can do a lot.

CHAPTER 3

THE SNOWBALL

Compound Earnings

One of the secrets to successful long term investing is the power of compound earnings. This means that you not only earn on the amount of your investment, but its earnings also start to earn. The most familiar form of compound earnings is the compound interest we get on bank deposits, but the principle is equally applicable to other kinds of earnings, such as dividends. We all know what compound interest is, at least in theory. We know it is better than simple interest, but most people don't appreciate its power, especially over the long term.

School Days

I can remember being taught that with interest compounded annually at 6%, for each dollar deposited I would get $.06 in interest the first year and $.0636 the second year, and so on. Big deal! But an investment is like a snowball. A small snowball, rolled in the snow picks up a little more snow on each revolution, enough to cover its circumference. At each revolution it becomes larger and collects more snow. Eventually each revolution collects many times more snow than the original ball.

How the Snowball works

The following table shows how larger amounts fare over a long period of time that would be characteristic of a long-term investment. We also get a little extra break since computers make it easy to compound continuously instead of annually.

TABLE 4
Compound Interest on $10,000 at Various Rates and Terms

RATE	3%	5%	10%	12%	14%
Deposit	10,000	10,000	10,000	10,000	10,000
5 Years	11,593	12,763	16,105	17,623	19,254
10 Years	13,439	16,289	25,937	31,058	37,072
20 Years	18,061	26,533	67,265	96,463	137,434
30 Years	24,273	43,219	174,494	299,599	509,502

I chose 3 to 14% growth rates because they bracket a large percentage of the rates earned on investments. I chose 12% to demonstrate once more the great difference that even 2% can make over many years. Even with an investment of just $10,000, the difference between 12% and 14% amounts to an astounding $209,903 in 30 years. This is incentive enough to look for even the slightest edge. It is also impressive how one investment of $10,000 with no additional contributions can snowball.

A regular investment program is even better

The figures in Table 2, however impressive, do not portray a typical long-term investment program. Average investors will start out with nothing and will make regular contributions from their income. Suppose that for 30 years you were to make contributions to your investment program of $200 per month. How would that come out?

TABLE 5
A Savings Program with Contributions of $200 per month - Humanity's Greatest Invention

Growth Rate	5%	10%	12%	14%
5 Years	13,658	15,616	16,247	17,440
10 Years	31,186	41,318	46,468	52,418
20 Years	82,549	153,139	199,830	263,269
30 Years	167,145	455,865	705,983	1,111,411

This is better but still not completely realistic. It would be normal for investors to increase their contributions to match inflation or their increasing income rather than a fixed $200 each month. In that case the final value might be two or three times as much. An important thing to notice is that while the interest rate does not make much difference the first 5 years, when you get to 30 years the difference is tremendous. This is because, at the start, the greatest contribution to the fund is the monthly payment, but gradually that changes and the greatest contribution is the interest itself. In the last month of the 30 years the growth of the 14% fund is 65 times the $200 contribution. It is no wonder that many investors consider that humankind's most important invention was not fire or the wheel, but compound interest.

It is easy to see that compounding is one of the main factors in long term investing. Table 5 shows what a regular, but fairly modest savings plan can accomplish. By saving $2,400 a year for 30 years, you have contributed $72,000 but you may very well wind up with 15 times that much.

The Importance of an Early Start

One point I want to stress is the effect of time in this computation. You may think, "The amount I can afford to put away now is insignificant. In five years I shall be able to set aside a respectable amount. I guess I shall start then." Aside from the very real danger that you might again put it off, how much difference does an early start make?

TABLE 6

Result of a One Time Investment of $100 @ 12% When you reach Age 65

Savers Age	Amount Invested	Number of years invested	Value at Age 65
2 0	$ 1 0 0	4 5	1 6 ,3 9 9
2 5	$ 1 0 0	4 0	9 ,3 0 5
3 0	$ 1 0 0	3 5	5 ,2 7 6
3 5	$ 1 0 0	3 0	2 ,9 9 6
4 0	$ 1 0 0	2 5	1 ,7 0 0
4 5	$ 1 0 0	2 0	9 6 5
5 0	$ 1 0 0	1 5	5 4 7
5 5	$ 1 0 0	1 0	3 1 1
6 0	$ 1 0 0	5	1 7 6

The amount you can save may seem hardly worth while.   But if you start early, it will eventually amount to a substantial sum. One hundred dollars saved at 20 is almost equal to a thousand at 40 and ten thousand at 60. But there is a little good news for the procrastinator. Even at age 50, with 15 years to go, you wind up with more than 5 times your original investment. Of course these are just one-time investments. A saver would add regularly. Looking at it another way, suppose you decide that when you retire at age 65 you want to have $1,000,000. How much would you have to put aside each month depending on your age when you start?

TABLE 7

Monthly Contribution Invested @ 12% to Make $1 Million at Age 65

Age at Start	Number of Years Invested	Monthly Payment
20	45	$46
30	35	154
40	25	527
50	15	1,982
60	5	12,123

Starting at age 20 the project is relatively painless, less than $1.50 per day. If an investor were to increase contributions to match pay increases, he or she could accumulate 2 or 3 million. Even at age 30 it is not too burdensome, but after that it ranges from difficult to impossible. Moral: Start early.

CHAPTER 4

INFLATION

Another Kind of Snowball

Compounding is like a two edged sword, it cuts both ways. When you are winning it gives you a lift, but when you are in trouble it works against you. Interest on your debt snowballs the same way as earnings do, except faster because the rate is higher. At least it is possible to avoid this by staying out of debt. There is one kind of negative compounding that we can not prevent, inflation. We have to learn to deal with it. We can not stop the rain, but we can buy an umbrella. Even so we should heed the warning of a poet whose name I know not.

> The rain it raineth everywhere,
>
> Upon the just and unjust fella,
>
> But more upon the just, because
>
> The unjust stole the just's umbrella.

The Worker Can Keep Pace

I recently heard a young financial reporter say that the current inflation rate of 3% is no problem, it is negligible. It is true that for most workers our chronic inflation is a minor nuisance, because wages and prices, as a whole, increase at about the same rate. This is very uneven though, medical costs are up sharply and long distance telephone rates have plunged. It is irritating to see prices endlessly creeping upward. For many, however, because they are climbing the ladder, they can put up with moderate inflation. But it takes a lot of the fun out of it when they realize that the increased pay doesn't provide a higher living standard but just keeps them even. Well, it could be worse and when you retire, it will be.

The Retiree Cannot

For most people, inflation has little effect on their daily lives, but there is a growing segment of the population that is in a real bind. These are the retirees living on incomes that are either fixed or are increasing more slowly than inflation. We have just reviewed the power of compounding and how helpful it can be to our investment program. If your savings are eroding from inflation, the losses compound. And this back edge of compounding's sword wounds retirees and slowly drains away the life-blood of their savings. The bad news is that, with any luck, you will some day retire. But, recognizing this problem in advance, you have a fighting chance to cope with it.

An Integral Part of Retirement Planning

In planning for retirement, it is vital to make full provision for the ravages of inflation. Comparison of the following tables will show you how a sum of money that seems adequate today may fall far short by the time you retire.

TABLE 8

A Savings Program With Contributions of $200 per Month With Adjustments for 3.1% Inflation

Growth Rate	10%	Adjusted 3.1 10%	14%	Adjusted 3.1 14%
5 Years	15,616	14,364	17,440	16,005
10 Years	41,318	34,625	52,418	43,541
20 Years	153,139	103,521	263,269	172,407
30 Years	455,865	240,610	1,111,411	553,810

Taking the Fun Away

In 30 years you have contributed $72,000. And at a nominal rate of 10%, which is 6.91% after correcting for inflation, and even at a nominal 14%, the gain looks pretty anemic after inflation. You may be surprised to see that while the differences in the totals are quite small at 5 years, they become greater and greater as time goes on. As we saw before in the chapter on compounding, this is the snowball effect of interest earning interest, and you will notice the same thing in many of the subsequent tables. This is a battle between the negative compounding of inflation and the positive compounding of earnings. To win this battle, the positive growth of your investments must be substantially greater than the negative erosion of inflation. The greater the difference, the better.

Shot in the Foot

The cruelest thing is that the unsophisticated investors, who are the great majority of those getting hurt, never realize what hit them. They think it was inflation, while the real cause was their own failure to recognize the danger and prepare for it. They never heard the saying "We have met the enemy, and it is us."

The Melting Nest Egg

Inflation not only makes it more difficult to accumulate an adequate nest egg, but it should not surprise you to hear that it will continue to erode it for the rest of your life in retirement. This could easily last 30 years or more. Let us see what can happen to an unwary retiree who takes a $200,000 lump sum payment in lieu of a pension. He is careful and "conservative" and invests it in what he is told is the safest possible way, 30 year 7% U. S. Treasury Bonds. With the $14,000 income from the company and his Social Security, he thinks he has provided well for his future. The following Table shows the result.

TABLE 9

Effect of 3.1% Inflation on the Purchasing Power of a 7% Treasury Bond (Principal & Income)
High Hopes Gone Sour

Time	Value of Principal	Value of Income
At Start	200,000	14,000
5 Years	170,863	11,960
10 Years	145,971	10,218
15 Years	124,706	8,729
20 Years	106,538	7,458
30 Years	77,758	5,443

This man retired at age 62. Now, at age 92, he has lost much of the value of his pension. Inexperienced himself, he relied on almost the worst possible advice, that this was the safest and most conservative place to put his money. He has become almost a pauper. Was this a "safe" investment for this retiree? Did it "conserve" his assets? He was already in a bad spot with an inadequate nest egg, then acting on bad advice, he made a difficult situation much worse. We will explore ways to avoid or minimize such problems.

CHAPTER 5

RISK AND OPPORTUNITY

Risk is a Bad Word

This word is scary. It is overused and misused. Risk is the chance that something bad will happen. We certainly want to be aware of risks and plan so that we can minimize them, but over emphasis on risk creates a distorted image of the investment environment. After all, there is also the chance that something good will happen. In fact, when you consider the stock market as a place to invest, good things are twice as frequent as bad. I am sure a psychologist would know why there is no word the exact opposite to risk in meaning. The best we can do is the neutral word chance.

Living with Risk

We can not get rid of the word but maybe, if we have a better understanding of what it means, we can put it in a more realistic perspective. Risk is as familiar to us as the air we breathe. We all take hundreds of risks every day. Most of them are almost automatic. For example when we drive to work there is perhaps, one chance in a million that we will die in a traffic accident. That is bad, but if we do not go to work, we face the risk of losing our job, which is also bad. By not going to work, we eliminate one risk and incur a different one. It is usual, although we often do not realize it, that when we eliminate one risk, we incur a different one. Once we decide that going to work is the better alternative, we don't have to figure that out every day. It just becomes routine. Some risks are very small, but the penalty for loss is so severe that we don't take them, like the risk of our house burning down. We insure it. Other risks are very great but the penalty for loss is slight, and we often take that risk, like leaving the raincoat home when rain threatens. So we are accustomed to weighing risks, even in matters of life and death, and deciding which to take, and what other risk we would get in its place. As an investor you will go through the same process. You will weigh the alternatives and accept the one that is the least unfavorable.

Uncertainty = Opportunity

Uncertainty is a more useful concept than risk. Life is uncertain, which is one of its best features. Think how deadly life would be if it were nothing but a predictable routine. While bad things can happen, good things are just as likely. Instead of breaking your leg today, you might meet a beautiful person. Another way of looking at uncertainty is to look at the odds. This is the businesslike approach: get in a position where the odds are in your favor, and the longer those odds, the better. This is the way you will approach investments. Nothing will be absolutely certain, but, by careful consideration of the odds and by making choices that make them work in your favor, you can come close to certainty of success.

What are the Risks for an Investor?

1. The first is the **Business Risk**, the loss of all or part of your investment, because a company's business becomes less successful than expected.

2. One, widely ignored, is the **Inflation Risk**. This is what happens when the dollar loses value and the dollars you have saved will not buy as much as when they were invested.

3. Another one, somewhat similar, is the **Interest Rate Risk.** When short-term interest rates decline sharply, it can have a devastating effect on unwary investors. It creates particular difficulty for retirees who often rely on bonds, CDs, the money market, annuities, and other sources of interest income for their living expenses. People who have bonds that are not due for some years and pay a higher interest rate feel safe. However, many such bonds contain a provision that they can be paid off before maturity at the issuer's option. If interest rates go down the issuer is very likely to redeem the high interest bonds and reissue new ones at a lower rate. This is a serious risk.

4. There is also a **Market Risk**. If the stock market suffers a general decline, it will usually affect the price of most stocks, and even if a company is still doing very well, the price of its stock may temporarily decline significantly. This does not affect earnings or dividends or the fundamental value of the company. For a long-term investor, since he has no intention to sell and since the long term trend is still up, this is mainly an opportunity to buy high quality stocks at bargain prices. For a short term investor who needs the cash this may have a severe effect.

5. A risk that I particularly dislike is the **Liquidity Risk.** The kinds of stocks you will invest in are publicly traded and can be sold, during business hours, in 5 minutes for a fair price, and liquidity is no problem. But small companies, especially local businesses, including small banks, may not be listed on any exchange, and may be difficult to sell except at a deep discount. Also real estate, antiques, and other material objects may take months or years to sell at a fair value.

6. The **Regulatory Risk** is often difficult to evaluate. This includes not only existing regulation, like the public service commission's control over public utilities, but unexpected regulations and restrictions that can be imposed by legislation or executive order on virtually any business. This is not as bad

as it sounds because, with the possible exception of the tobacco industry, no one wants to drive companies out of business.

7. The Worst Risk Of All - **Rust and Dust**. This is a sneaky clandestine risk which does more damage than all the others combined. I have never heard it described as a risk, but you had better pay attention to it. It is the risk of low profitability, the risk of stagnation, of being left at the post. Risk is the chance something bad will happen. Low profitability is bad, and when compounded over the years, it becomes a disaster, and it will surely happen to you unless you see the danger clearly and take effective action to forestall it. Rust and dust is worse than wear and tear. Do not think your broker, adviser, or mutual fund will protect you. You must take charge. A lot more about this as we go along.

The Danger of Tunnel Vision

The most important thing an investor should know about risk is that, contrary to popular belief, there is no such thing as a risk free investment. We live in an environment of risk. It is present in everything we do, and in every investment, whether a Bangladesh Ski Resort or U.S. Treasury Bonds. Risks come in different shapes and sizes, but you can be sure they are always there. To avoid the risks that are the most harmful, you must evaluate the alternatives. Sometimes people worry about risks that are negligible. As an example, an astronomer in a lecture commented that eventually, perhaps in 50 billion years, our sun would explode consuming the earth, extinguishing all life. An elderly lady, greatly agitated, waved her arm to ask a question, "How long did you say before this will happen?" "Fifty billion years." he replied. "Thank heaven", said the woman, "I thought you said 50 <u>million</u>." People often consider only one type of risk and, in avoiding that one, blunder into something worse. Before committing to any investment make sure you understand its potential problems.

How to Manage Risk

If there is a risk you must take, one way to control it is by diluting it, by diversification. This is how insurance companies, who are in the risk business, manage their risks. They do not just insure one house against fire, they insure thousands. One or two will burn, but the premiums paid by the others will cover the costs with a little to spare. This same method is available to investors. The chance of a strong company going bad is small, but if you invest in 10 or 15 strong companies in different industries, that is your insurance. If one company is disappointing or even two, the good results of the rest will more than make up for that. You will see an actual example of how this works in a future chapter. This is diversification and is an indispensable ingredient of any stock portfolio.

Don't Fear Risk

Risk isn't all bad. Sometimes it may be another name for opportunity. If a risk would tilt the odds against you, don't take it. Buy something where the risk is manageable and you can arrange the odds in your favor.

CHAPTER 6

Rational Market or Happy Hunting Ground?

An Economic Theory

There is an economic theory that people are rational beings and, in the long run will, either consciously or subconsciously, make decisions that are in their best interests. So what? What has that to do with our investment strategy? The reason, as we shall soon see, is that our success as investors will be substantially affected by the behavior of the mass of investors and they will act very differently if the theory is correct than if it is flawed. This theory sounds reasonable and it has very impressive support. We all know that the ability to reason is what separates us from the beasts and furthermore the U S Constitution states that all men are created equal. But it is still just a theory and until it is tested by fire and is proven true, we do not want to bet the ranch on it.

The Rational Market

If the theory were valid, the buyers and sellers, as they mutually agreed on the value of a stock, would soon establish its true worth. With occasional temporary aberrations, all stocks would be valued on the same scale. There would be no bargains and all investors would do equally well. However, if it should turn out that investors in general are considering factors that have little or no effect on the value of stocks, the market is, to some degree, irrational and some stocks are over or under valued, creating an opportunity for a smart investor.

Irrational Advice

I believe that there is conclusive, in fact overwhelming, evidence that investors, usually with professional advice, habitually make irrational investment decisions, and these decisions display recognizable patterns. While I do not want to get ahead of myself, because we will study this matter in detail later, I want to present now a brief outline of my conclusions.

The Timid Grasshopper

I believe that all humans have an innate tendency to be timid. Our remote ancestors were no match, physically, for a saber toothed tiger or other large predators, but they were smarter. Timidity, or excessive caution, was a useful trait for survival. Of course many people have this under control, but most people are timid, especially in unfamiliar surroundings like the stock market. Anything that moves makes them nervous. Another human weakness is the tendency to place a higher value on instant gratification than on future security. These tendencies and others that I will discuss later cause the majority of investors to favor securities for reasons unrelated to their long range potential. This endless supply of irrational decisions provides rich opportunities for smart investors.

The Flaw in the Theory

While I do not deny that humans have the ability to reason, the theory, at least in its application to the market, does not take into account that the ability to reason is not absolute. This talent is not distributed evenly. It is like common sense. Some have a greater aptitude than others have. Even the greatest thinkers may goof occasionally. It has happened to me once or twice. Well, we do not have to worry about theories, we can just be thankful that, for some reason, we are given a happy hunting ground.

CHAPTER 7

The New Conservatives

Meet the World's Most Conservative Investor

That is I. I invest only in the common stock of a diversified selection of the most solid and most profitable companies in the world. They are U S companies, usually with world-wide interests, that have operated profitably often for 50 to 100 years and more. I almost never sell, but occasionally add to my holdings when I have saved a few thousand dollars. These investments provide a good income, which increases by about 8% each year, and the value of the capital also achieves substantial growth. Could there be a safer, more comfortable, or in other words a more conservative way to invest?

A New Language

And yet, your broker, banker, or adviser would describe my portfolio as aggressive, risky. "Conservative" to them is investing in bonds or CDs which as long-term investments are much riskier than high grade stocks. Why such a radical difference of opinion? Actually there is not so much a difference of opinion as a difference of language. Whenever you deal with these professionals you should be aware that they use a jargon in which plain English words have meanings unrelated to their use in standard English.

Is it Imagination?

But can a market be risky? Is this just imaginary? Not at all, it is possible to take dangerous risks in the stock market and everywhere else. It happens every day. Does this mean you will be in danger? Well consider this analogy. A bread knife is very sharp. It is risky to use. You can cut off your finger. If it were dull, it would not cut your finger, nor slice bread either. With reasonable care you can slice bread safely, and the same thing is true of investing in stocks.

Businesslike Approach

You are going to be handling your own affairs, and especially your retirement savings program. You will be operating a small, but a very important business. You should recognize this, and conduct it in a strictly businesslike way. Let us start now and examine the nature of fixed income investments, which include bonds, bank deposits, CDs, Money Markets, mortgages, and other securities that pay interest income. These are all, in one way or other, loans. The money, valued in dollars, is always yours. You merely lend it to a person, a bank, a corporation, or a governmental agency for temporary use. The borrower agrees to pay rent (interest) while using it. The borrower will repay the exact number of dollars borrowed at a specified future date. If it is for a short period, of 30, 60, or 90 days, inflation is probably negligible. However, if the term of the loan is for a period of years, sometimes as long as 30 years, you have handed the borrower dollars that were worth 100 cents. The ones he hands back may be worth one third as much as the ones you loaned, having lost two thirds of their purchasing power. And this would also be true if there were a succession of loans over that period instead of one. This devaluation of a lifetime of savings is a rude shock when you come to retire.

Who is to Blame?

The first question is, "Who did this to me?" It must have been the politicians, or big business, or the bankers, or any other favorite scapegoat. It surely could not have been the victim's fault - could it? This question and the answer illustrate a common human failing that makes it harder to solve problems, passing the buck - avoiding the blame. First, it is well known that, if you ask the wrong question, you are very likely to get the wrong answer. The right question here is, "What could I have done differently to avoid this loss?" If you ask this question you won't waste time and energy trying to fix the blame elsewhere. My most important message, and you will find it in every element of this book, is that YOU, and nobody else, are responsible for your success or failure. Inflation Risk is one of the factors that makes bonds and other fixed income investments unsafe and unsuitable for long term investments. In a sense this isn't even a risk. It is a GUARANTEED LOSS. A friend of mine, who is an investment professional, refers to bonds as "certificates of confiscation".

You are the Trustee

To me, money is a little different from other kinds of property. It is very powerful and yet it can vanish like a wet pavement in the sun. I feel more like the custodian of my assets rather than a proprietor. I respect it for what it can do, but if it is to accomplish anything, it must be protected. We don't always think of it that way, but with the accumulation of money comes the responsibility to take care of it and use it responsibly. Whether the ultimate purpose is for retirement or to benefit heirs, the trustee or custodian of assets should invest prudently. Think of yourself as a trustee. You will be held accountable for your stewardship.

Tracing the Dollars

We can get a better understanding of our small business of handling our assets if we follow the course of these dollars we lend. Suppose you loan your money to a bank. Depending whether it is a deposit or a CD, the bank will generally pay you annual interest of between 1% and 5%. It is a toss-up whether the interest will keep up with inflation. In many cases you are actually losing money instead of earning it when you lend it. This would be the case if you were getting 2% interest while inflation was eroding the value of your capital at a rate of 3%. What then, will the bank do with your dollars? It will lend them to someone else, someone who will pay it more than it's paying you, perhaps somewhere between 8 1/2% and 13%. The bank is making more on this deal than you are, and it is using your money.

The Second Borrower

Who is this second borrower, and what does she do with the money? This second borrower is a businesswoman, and she wants to modernize her plant. She manufactures widgets, and with the planned improvements, she can make twice as many widgets for a little more than her present costs. She is paying perhaps 9% interest, but she figures that the increased profit will be at least 18% of the value of the loan, so she, too, is making twice as much as you are, again on your money.

Who is in the Wrong Business?

Hold on, just a MINUTE! Eighteen percent? I am making 1% or possibly 5% at best, maybe not even keeping up with inflation. The bank, with **my** money, is making as much or more, less expenses, and the businesswoman, still with my money, is making another 9%. I am in the wrong business. In the first place, I could loan the money directly to the businesswoman and double, triple, or quadruple my income, but, if I owned the business, I would get the full value of my money, maybe 18%.

Where the Action is

It is clear that business is where the action is. The interest you can get depends on the health of business. The lender can not get more than some fraction of the business profit. Interest rates fluctuate, but on the whole, they can never come close to the business profit. It does not take an economist or a mathematician to figure out that there is more profit in operating a business than in loaning money to it - a LOT more profit. In the chapter on inflation we saw the disastrous effect of long term inflation on the value of the dollar and consequently on bonds and other fixed income securities. As you can now see, that was only half the story. Even if inflation should disappear for good, the inherent low profitability of interest bearing securities makes them unsuitable for long term investment. This fact is often unknown to unsophisticated investors who are apt to look only at the income, not realizing that most companies pay out less than half their earnings, reinvesting the rest in the business and increasing the value of the stock. As an example one stock that I hold has increased in value 9 times in the past 15 years. This is not at all unusual and shows why I do not buy bonds.

How to Get Into Business

You could start a business of your own, which is risky, and it would take a lot of time and energy. But, as you surely know already, it is possible to buy shares in an existing business. To make it easier for investors to buy and sell shares, there are stock exchanges whose principal business is to facilitate stock transactions. You can easily, and at very little expense, become part owner of the strongest and most profitable companies in the world. More detailed information later.

A Secular Trend

We have reviewed some of the underlying principles and the forces that we can use to our advantage in managing our long-term assets. There is one more that is of vital importance in our selection of investments. The New York Stock Exchange has recently celebrated its 200th anniversary, and a study of stock prices over that whole period shows a strong, and consistent upward trend, which is substantially greater than inflation. There have, of course, been ups and downs. It is a saw-tooth curve, and a short-term investment can result in a loss, but in the long run the chance for success is very good indeed. This trend is illustrated on the following chart.

FIGURE 1

This is great for a 200-year investment, but how has it done lately? **Ibbotson Associates**, a well known and highly respected research firm, has made a detailed study of the performance of different types of investment for the past 70 years. They have computed the present value of one dollar invested on 12/31/25 with all income reinvested. They selected the favorite investments, Treasury Bills, Long Term Government Bonds, Large company stocks, and Small Company Stocks.

The results are shown in the following table:

Table 10
12/31/95 Value of $1 Invested 12/31/25 All Income Reinvested

Type of Investment	% Total Return	Total Value
Small Company Stocks	12.5	$3,822
Large Company Stocks	10.5	1,114
Long Term government Bonds	5.2	34
U. S. Treasury Bills	3.7	13
Inflation	3.1	8.58

© Ibbotson Associates

How about the Small Cap Stocks?

At first glance, Small Company Stocks look very, very good. You might be thinking, "That is the way to go!" But there are a few problems. It is difficult for the average investor to get enough information about many of them, and while the <u>average</u> does remarkably well, many of them do poorly or even fail, so, to get a good cross section you might have to buy 100 or more companies. You would have a lot of bookkeeping and performance tracking to do, and it still might not work out too well. There are mutual funds that specialize in these stocks. How about them? There is one fly in that ointment. You will note that the small cap stocks do 2% better than the large stock average, but mutual funds charge management fees, perhaps about 3%. This would more than wipe out the advantage. It is safer not to be too greedy. The common stocks of the S&P 500 do very well, although you will probably do even better.

What does this Ibbotson Study Mean to Us?

First of all, it confirms and reinforces our theoretical conclusions about the investment value of bonds for the long term. In spite of its great importance to investors, this study is not exactly news. Savvy investors (a very small minority, which you will soon join) have known for many years that bonds are poor long-term investments. Although the superiority of stocks as a long-term investment has been well known, nevertheless, this study furnishes solid confirmation and has convinced many who had been uncertain. While many advisers, and many investors, still cling to bonds, it is no longer a sacrilege to give preference to stocks. The staggering difference after 70 years is another graphic illustration of the miserable performance of <u>all</u> the securities dependent on interest income - money loaned - over the long term. But 70 years is a very long time, and due to the powerful magic of compounding, the differences it shows, while mathematically correct, are much greater than would show up in the life of the usual savings program of 30 years, or so. When we use Ibbotson's growth rates but shorten the term to 30 years, we get the following results:

TABLE 11
Total Return From $1 Investment After 30 Years Using the same growth rates as the Ibbotson Report

Type of Investment	% Total Return	Total Value
Small Company Stocks	12.5	$34.24
Large Company Stocks	10.5	19.99
Long Term government Bonds	5.2	4.58
U. S. Treasury Bills	3.7	2.97
Inflation	3.1	2.5

© Ibbotson Associates

Still the Same Answer

While the differences are very much smaller than in the 70 year study, the conclusion is loud and clear, the prudent investor should never include fixed income securities as any part of a long term investment portfolio! The reason for emphasizing the point so strongly is that the myth of bonds as a safe and conservative investment is so strongly entrenched, there is a tradition that brokers and advisers, who really know better, will recommend some arbitrary percentage of bonds and cash automatically "for safety". For the long term this is complete nonsense. Funds you will need for contingencies or for some special short-term purpose should be liquid, some type of cash equivalent. But this has nothing to do with your investment program and the amount should be based on your needs, not as an arbitrary percentage of your assets.

Difference Understated

These stocks in Ibbotson's study were a kind of market cross section and not a selection of the best. They were not managed by weeding out the substandard performers. A carefully selected and managed portfolio, such as yours will be, would surely do at least 2% better. We have seen what even such a small increase means in the long run.

One Question

If business is so much more profitable than lending, how come dividends are lower than interest rates? Well, the profitability of stock as measured in the Ibbotson study is made up of two components. The first is the increase in the price of the stock, called "appreciation", and this is the most important. The reason for this increase in value is the company's growth and the fact that a large share of its earnings, usually more than half, is plowed back into the business each year. The second component is the income, the dividend that would be paid to the investor. Bonds pay out all their earnings but have no growth in value, which is more important in the long run.

Why do Stocks Grow?

Although a company's profits all belong to the shareholders, a company almost never pays out all its earnings in dividends. It is apt to pay out a bit less than half, and sometimes much less. These retained earnings are used to improve the company's future earnings. This practice is beneficial to the stockholders, especially for long term investors. First, while you pay income tax on the dividends you receive, you do not pay on the retained earnings. The second advantage is that these funds may grow rapidly due to a combination of good management and the compounding effect.

What has it done for us Lately?

The Ibbotson study started a long time ago and covers a longer period than most investment programs. Of interest are the present and some specific stocks as examples. I made such a study in June 1991 for the period June 1, 1981 to June 1, 1991, and then updated it to June 1, 1996. I selected 10 stocks that I personally held during that period. I think it is a fair sample of what any experienced investor might have selected on June 1, 1981. I made up a phantom portfolio of about $10,000 in each stock, and followed them for ten years. Here is the portfolio at the start.

TABLE 12
Portfolio of High Grade Stocks Performing Over 10 Years
Selected June 1, 1981

Company	# Shares	Cost per share	Annual Income	Total Value
American Home Prod	300	34	570	10,200
Cons Paper	300	34	600	10,200
Deluxe Corp	175	59	263	10,325
R. R. Donnelley	250	39	320	9,750
Exxon	150	65	900	9,750
General Electric	150	67	474	10,050
Heinz	185	54	266	9,990
Marsh & McClennan	280	36	560	10,080
Merck	100	100	252	10,000
Philip Morris	180	52	360	9,350
TOTAL			4,565	99,705

For Comparison
U.S.Treasury Bond $100,000 @ 7%   Income = $7,000

As planned it totals about $100,000 in stocks and, for comparison, an equal investment in a 7% U.S. Treasury Bond. To many investors the bond would be more attractive because of the higher income and the misconception that bonds are safer. But let us see what these investments look like 10 years later.

TABLE 13

Status June 1, 1991

Company	# Shares	Cost per share	Annual Income	Total Value	Annual Return
American Home Prod	600	59	1,428	35,400	17.3
Cons Paper	1200	41	1,536	49,200	20.1
Deluxe Corp	770	43	893	33,110	15.1
R. R. Donnelley	1000	49	1000	49,000	19.5
Exxon	600	58	1,608	34,800	18.1
General Electric	600	77	1,248	46,200	19.1
Heinz	1110	38	1,166	42,180	18.3
Marsh & McClennan	560	78	1,456	43,680	19.1
Merck	600	119	1,380	71,400	24.7
Philip Morris	1440	68	2,750	97,920	29.3
TOTAL			14,465	505,890	20.7

U.S.Treasury Bond @ 7%   Annual Income = $7,000 $100,000   Annual 7.0%

These are real figures of real life stocks. In 10 years the total value has increased to more than 5 times the original investment, and, incidentally, this is <u>without</u> any income reinvestment. And the stockholder's income is more than twice that of the bondholder, and the difference will accelerate as time goes on. One caution however, this decade was extraordinarily profitable for stocks. While the increase in income is about what you might expect, the value of the stocks would normally about triple in ten years. Even at triple, however, the stock performance makes the bonds look sick, especially when comparing the income, supposedly one of bonds' best features. This is only a ten-year study, but you know enough about compounding to realize that a thirty year comparison would be dramatic.

The Payoff

The real payoff, however, is shown in the last column, the total return. This includes not only the dividends paid but the increase in value of the shares as well. This is clearer when shown in tabular form.

TABLE 14

Ten Year Results

	Amount of Investment	Annual Income	10 Years Income	10 Year Appreciation	Total Ten Year Return
Bond	$100,000	$7,000	$70,000	0	$70,000
Stock	99,705	9,515(est)	95,150	406,185	501,335

I estimated the stock income as an average of the first and last year, but, no matter how you figure it, the difference is overwhelming.

One thing might cause a little confusion. At first glance it appears that for most of these stocks the share prices are lower than they were 10 years before. The reason is that the stocks have split and the investor has many more shares now than which he started.

Update

Since June 1991 it has not been all smooth sailing. We had a short but troublesome recession and we had governmental attacks of unprecedented severity on the pharmaceutical and tobacco industries, which sharply affected three stocks in our portfolio. The passage of time and a strong stock market after the recession has restored these companies to financial health. The tobacco industry, however, is still under heavy and persistent attack, but so far it has proved exceptionally resilient. One of our companies was hurt badly. It just happens to be in the wrong business at the wrong time. Deluxe Checkprinters, now Deluxe Corporation, has suffered a sharp decrease in demand for its principal product and, at the same time, faces increased competition. Even so, the company has remained profitable, though without the growth formerly achieved.

The Result

You might expect this series of misfortunes to three of the ten companies in the study would wound it severely. Let's see what actually happened.

TABLE 15

Status June 1, 1996 - after 15 years

Company	# Shares	Cost per share	Annual Income	Total Value	Annual Return
American Home Prod	1200	54	1,848	64,800	16.1
Cons Paper	1200	52	2,016	62,400	15.8
Deluxe Corp	700	36	1,036	25,200	10.2
R. R. Donnelley	2000	37	1,440	74,000	16.5
Exxon	600	85	1,896	51,000	15.4
General Electric	1200	83	2,208	99,600	18.7
Heinz	1665	33	1,765	54,945	15.2
Marsh & McClennan	560	94	1,792	52,640	15.1
Merck	1800	65	2,448	117,000	19.9
Philip Morris	1440	99	5,760	142,560	23.9
TOTAL			14,465	505,890	17.1

U.S.Treasury Bond @ 7%   Annual Income = $7,000 $100,000   Annual 7.0%

Surprise!

In spite of the recession, the portfolio grew by 58% while the income has increased almost as much, by 41%. The three stocks that were under attack, American Home, Merck, and Philip Morris, temporarily slipped below the June 1991 levels but have recovered very well. Deluxe, however has continued to slip. But what can we learn from the progress of this portfolio?

Lesson #1

Even in a selected group of high-grade growth stocks there will be a wide variation in performance. After many years of exceptional growth some companies gradually slow down, others have a temporary problem and resume their growth pattern, and some just go flat. This does not mean they are failing or going broke, but it means they no longer support our objectives. It is important to keep track of our stocks, and it is often hard to decide whether it is a temporary problem or whether the company has run out of gas. This is very important because it is frustrating to sell and pay a high tax on capital gains and then see the company revive and forge ahead. I have had that painful experience, but in this portfolio we would have been better off to sell several of the slower movers.

Lesson #2

Diversification helps cushion the effects of adversity. As some stocks had problems, others took up the slack. And even during the recession the value of the portfolio and its income continued to grow.

Lesson #3

Do not give up on a strong company. Two of the strongest are Merck and Philip Morris. Both were heavily battered. Both companies are extremely strong financially and even when their stock prices fell, they continued to profit and increased their dividends. If a company's sales and earnings are healthy, it is a keeper. Of course Philip Morris is a special problem. The government may eventually prevail, but I would not bet on it. It will not be easy to skin that bear.

Lesson #4

The most important lesson is the overwhelming superiority of common stocks over bonds. It is only a slight exaggeration to say that the worst stock is better than the best bond. The total stock portfolio is now worth more than 7 times the value of the bonds and the income is nearly triple. Even the lowest of the stocks is worth 2½ times the equivalent bond's value. The best is worth 14 times as much and yields more than 8 times as much.

Confirming Ibbotson

These results are thoroughly consistent with the Ibbotson study, and they confirm that the trend it shows is still with us. But the total return of these stocks, at 17.1%, is almost double that of Ibbotson's large stocks, which averaged 10.5%. I attribute the difference to two factors. Ten years of my fifteen-year study were exceptionally favorable for stocks. You could not hope to achieve such a result over an extended period of years. In addition when I selected these stocks, I chose what I considered the cream of the crop, while Ibbotson's sample was the entire S&P 500. If investors can pick superior stocks by careful selection, and I am sure they can, their results ought to be better than Ibbotson's cross section.

The Next Question is Safety

Although it is clear that business can be much more profitable than lending, businesses sometimes fail, and even the strongest are not exempt from financial problems. How can you participate in business profits and still be safe? This portfolio provides an excellent answer. Here you have three companies in the drug and tobacco industries that had tough and unexpected regulatory problems. All are strong, and earnings are good and, though they were battered, they have weathered the storm very well. In strong companies deterioration takes a long, long time and sends out repeated warning signals. Investors have plenty of time to decide whether to sell or whether the company will recover. When you have owned shares in a company for several years and you begin to lose confidence in it, there is little chance that you will lose money when you sell. You are more likely to be faced with a capital gain. But, as a company continues to lag, the safe interval for a decision becomes shorter.

Time for Decision

Investment grade common stocks are safe, but safety is never absolute, you have to take reasonable precautions. A street may be safe, but not if you drive on the wrong side. With your investments, like your driving, you have to pay attention. Occasionally a fine strong company runs into trouble. One of the most prominent recent examples is IBM. It was probably the strongest and most successful company in the world and yet it suffered a disastrous collapse. How could share owners have protected themselves? In a later chapter I will discuss the IBM case in detail including the many years of storm signals before the crash, the errors made by many investors, and even analysts, and how I protected myself. There have been a few other cases and almost always plenty of advance warning. There is one thing that sometimes blinds investors - love. Never fall in love with a stock.

The Bottom Line

Past experience, confirmed by these studies, suggests that a conservative expectation for total return of a well-managed long term portfolio of common stocks is at least 12%. If this looks a little high compared to Ibbotson, remember that your selection of 10 or 15 stocks should do better than a cross section of 500. I also expect the inflation rate will continue to average about 3.1% for the foreseeable future. These are the assumptions I will generally use in this book.

The "New Conservatives"

Those who are cautious investors and want to preserve the value of their assets must redefine "conservative" as it applies to investing. Suppose every broker and every advisor calls bonds conservative, does that help you when you retire with most of your savings dissipated? Literally millions of people are suffering today because of this misconception. Millions more will suffer in the future. But neither you nor I have to participate in this fatal game. Join the NEW CONSERVATIVES and rely on your common sense instead of the tired and worn out mythology of the past.

CHAPTER 8

The Balanced Portfolio

In 1943 I was young, naive, and in the Navy. In those happy days, although I had been investing for nearly fifteen years, I had never heard of a Balanced Portfolio. But I was soon to experience its sting.

The Doubtful Beneficiary

In that year an uncle died and I became heir to 1/72 of his estate. In the many years that passed before the estate was finally settled, the trustee was the Comical Bank, or some similar name. The Trust Officer was a Mr. Procrustes and he sent me annual reports of the status of the trust. Mr. Procrustes lived by rigid rules and never deviated from his straight and narrow path. One of his rules was to maintain a fixed balance, I believe it was 50-50, between stocks and bonds. I noticed this because the stocks went up every year and the bonds went down. Instead of selling the bonds and buying more stock, Mr. Procrustes did his duty. Each year he balanced the portfolio by selling some of the good stocks and buying more of the bad bonds. I did not understand the finer points of trust management, and as a result carried on a spirited but fruitless correspondence with various bank officials. They were unmoved and the trust remained balanced until it was finally liquidated. I must be a slow learner, because I still do not see the profit in a continuing policy of reducing the best investments and increasing the worst.

Deja vu

For the next thirty years I was busy earning a living and saving for retirement, and I never heard a word about Balanced Portfolios, although I had not forgotten the Comical Bank. Gradually, however, I became aware that it was fashionable for brokers, advisers, and all manner of financial consultants to recommend the deplorable practice of investing long term assets in some arbitrary mixture of stocks and bonds, a balanced portfolio. This is where I came in. Yogi Berra had it right, this was déja vu all over again. Mr. Procrustes may be long gone, but his memory lingers on. After reading my previous warnings, and especially after digesting the report of the Ibbotson study, you might well wonder why all these professionals are so hot for bonds. I wonder the same thing. Why all these experts push bonds is an interesting question, but for the moment it is beside the point. For long-term investors the important question is whether this strategy will improve the performance or the safety of their portfolios.

A Dead Horse?

You may think I have spent enough time belaboring bonds. Why beat a dead horse? This horse is far from dead, he has more lives than a cat. Just today as I write this, 10,000 potential investors have been exposed to a pitch to buy bonds, and this is a Saturday. Of course I can not stem this tide, but I may be able to immunize some of my readers.

Wise(?) Counsel

In a recent article in the Wall Street Journal a staff reporter explained the advantages of a portfolio invested 60% in stocks and 40% in bonds or other fixed income securities. The main point seemed to be that this 60/40 balance must be maintained. This requires constant attention because stocks keep increasing in value but bonds do not. Of course this rebalancing is a nuisance. It is a lot of paper work. You pay commissions on the sales and purchases, you incur capital gains taxes, and you complicate your tax returns. The alleged benefit is that, in case the market suddenly dips 20%, you will be less vulnerable. For long-term inventors like us, what is this vulnerability?

The Answer

Considering Ibbotson's research, it doesn't seem logical that any long term portfolio would be improved by adding bonds. Although Ibbotson's presentation is compelling, it would be comforting to have independent confirmation. T. Rowe Price Associates, the big mutual fund manager, made a recent study. It analyzed the performance for the 48 year period from December 31, 1945 to December 31, 1993, of portfolios with various percentages of stocks and bonds. The results of this study, shown in Table 16, below, not only confirm Ibbotson but provide other useful information as well...

TABLE 16
T. Rowe Price Study   1945-93

Portfolio	Stocks	Bonds	Number of Down Years	Average Loss in down year	Worst One Year Loss	Average Total Return
Aggressive	100%	0%	11	-9.4%	-26.5%	11.7%
Growth	75%	25%	9	7.2	18.4	10.5
Balanced	50%	50%	8	-4	-10.4	9.1
Income	25%	75%	5	-1.5	-2.7	7.6
Conservative	0%	100%	5	-0.7	-1.3	5.9

© Wall Street Journal

Galloping Schizophrenia

This is a significant study. Its principal finding is that bonds, regardless of their percentage, always have a negative effect on long term investment. But its presentation is so slanted against stocks that a long-term investor does not know whether to laugh or cry. The emphasis is on some pretty scary statistics about "down years" and the worst year losses. The editor may admire "balance" in a portfolio, but it obviously has no place in this presentation. I would like to see equal emphasis on the number of "up" years, the average gain in those years, and the best one-year gain. And one more thing, we need a sharper focus on total return. The average investor cannot easily visualize the difference a couple of percentage points would mean in a 30 year savings program.

A Better Picture

The following table omits the misleading adjectives, aggressive, conservative, etc. It also shows the effect of differences in total return in your savings program when you come to retire.

TABLE 17
30 Year Program with Contributions of $200 per Month

Stock/Bond Ratio	Rate of Return	Final Balance	Total Contribution	Total Gain
100/0	11.7	660,415	72,000	588,415
75/25	10.5	507,684	72,000	435,684
50/50	9.1	376,702	72,000	304,702
25/75	7.6	276,688	72,000	204,688
0/100	5.9	198,072	72,000	126,072

The all stock portfolio winds up with more than three times that of the all bond portfolio but, since they both made the substantial contribution of $72,000, the stock fund had a gain nearly 5 times the bond fund. The Wall Street professionals who compiled this report can add and subtract as well as I can. They understand the difference between stocks and bonds, but they have a different objective. I am focused on the profit of long term investment. All I care about is the final result. They are concerned about the tender feelings of nervous investors. Nothing wrong with that but they should show the whole picture so the prospective investors could weigh the choice between being nervous now or after they retire.

A Prayer

If any of my readers still have an idea that some percentage of bonds is a good idea for long term investing, reread the chapter twice, and we will all pray for your speedy recovery.

CHAPTER 9

Speculation

Why talk about speculation? It is the antithesis of everything I have discussed in this book. The average individual investor would not have anything to do with speculation - would he?

A Common Weakness

Venture capitalist with tens, or hundreds of millions of dollars to invest, can prudently and profitably invest in companies whose chance of survival may be only one in ten. The secret is that they can invest in 100 or 1,000 such companies and if even a few hit the jackpot, it can be very profitable. While they are speculators, they may be a careful businesspeople who figure the odds and risks just as we do. For you or me, with limited capital, buying 2 or 3, or even a dozen stocks like these would be reckless gambling. The problem is that like the lottery, there are a few winners, and some of us are optimists. If you must gamble, I have a suggestion. Spend a dollar or two a week on a state lottery ticket. You probably won't win $10 million, but you will not lose tens of thousands either.

Jeopardizing Your Future

Foolish or not, a lottery ticket is a trivial thing, an investment gamble is a very different matter. In this case you are risking thousands or tens of thousands, which you could lose, with a potential, but unlikely, gain of probably 30% to 100%. This is your retirement fund, or a good chunk of it, that is at risk. How long will you live, especially how long will you live in retirement? I have already lived 23 years in retirement, and my prospective heirs fear that I may go another 10 or 15 years. This danger is illustrated by an irreverent poem:

> The animals are strictly dry,
> They sinless live and quickly die,
> But sinful, ginfull, rum soaked men
> Survive to four score years and ten.

And you, like me, being virtuous and temperate will probably last even longer. Thirty or forty years is a long, long time to live on short rations.

One Example

There are innumerable ways you can gamble in the stock market. Your broker is not likely to say to you, "Why not do a little gambling today?" The broker will suggest there is a good opportunity for profit. One of the common ways to gamble is to buy on margin. You have enough money to buy 1,000 shares of XYZ Biotek, which your broker thinks will go from 45 to 60 in the next 6 months. This would be a nice profit, but suppose you were to borrow enough from your broker to buy another thousand shares, your profit would double. Well, not exactly double, because you will have to pay interest on the money you have borrowed. Even so, your profit would increase substantially. That is, if all goes according to plan. That is the beauty of speculation: the optimism, the anticipation of fat profits. But we all know what happens to our best-laid plans. Suppose XYZ does not go up enough to pay the interest on your loan, or does not go up at all. You begin to develop a knot in your stomach. Do you hold on, losing money, hoping for a turn around? Worse yet, XYZ could go down. If you had bought just 1000 shares and paid for them, you could ride out the dip without discomfort. But the leverage that would have doubled your profit now is doubling your loss. This loss is continuing month after month, draining away the profits of your prudent investments, and you do not know when it will end or how much your total loss will be, because even if the stock goes to zero, you have to pay off your loan plus interest.

Another Way to Lose

A more risky gamble is to sell short. This time you think XYZ will go down, so you sell 200 shares that you do not own, promising you will deliver them at some future date. When it goes down enough you buy 200 shares at a lower price and deliver them to the buyer. But suppose the shares go up, you still have to buy the 200 shares and theoretically there is no limit to how high it can go. You could suffer a disastrous loss. And do not forget:

"He who sells what isn't his'n must buy it back or go to prison".

Commodities

Commodity and currency futures and stock options are also ways to bet on future price changes, but these markets are frequented by experts whose only business is trading in such markets. This is a different game. In the stock market everyone can win. If others are smarter than you, they will make more, but that will not affect you. This is a different matter. When one player wins, another loses. These traders know more than you do. You can guess who will be the loser. About ¾ of the dilettantes (average investors) lose. You do not want to buck these odds.

Speculation is Not Always a Gamble

There are some investments that would be wildly risky for us that have a sober business use. As an example, suppose that in May commodity traders believe that the price of corn in September will be $2.75 per bushel. Due to weather and market conditions, however, it might be $2.50 or $3. To farmers who will be ready to sell their crop at that time, the September price is important. A price of $2.50 might wipe out their profit for the year, while $3 would give them an exceptional profit. They can resolve the uncertainty by selling their crop now for September delivery. The miller and processor have the same problem in reverse. They would prefer to pay $2.50 but may well settle for the current price rather than take the chance it may go to $3.

Professionals Sometimes Lose Big

Investors with important money, perhaps more than $100 million, whether individuals, partnerships or funds, do not rest on their laurels. However much it is, they want to double it as quickly as possible. They are not satisfied with the normal 10% growth that we might find acceptable. They hire hot shot managers who develop exotic and ingenious strategies expected to return 15% or 20% per year, or even more. Investment contributions may total in the billions, and they borrow billions more to increase leverage. These are called Hedge Funds. Alas, even for these geniuses, things can go very wrong. While these high priced managers develop strategies that are more sophisticated and complex than the average investor, there is always an Achilles heel somewhere and, not surprisingly, the devices that sometimes generate super profits can also result in spectacular losses. Recently several of these Hedge Funds had to be liquidated resulting in billions of dollars in losses for the investors. This is an illustration that no one is so big or so smart that he is immune to risk. Whether a small individual or a giant fund, risky investments can be disastrous.

Injured Pride?

The investors can suffer serious losses. How about the advisers, the brokers, and fund managers, do they lose money in such a debacle? Of course there is nothing to prevent them from speculating but it makes more sense for them to stay on the sidelines and be satisfied with their fees and commissions. That way their only wound is to their pride. Surely few of these people are selling short, or buying on margin, or trading in futures. Their attitude toward speculation was expressed in three words by one of the world's greatest experts on gambling. Some time ago I saw a man, reputedly the king of bookmakers, being interviewed on TV. In response to a question he said that he never bet on a horse race. Why not? "You could lose."

Business or Speculation?

My wife is a goldsmith. When she started in business gold sold for about $50 an ounce. For some years its price increase was gradual, but suddenly it began to take off - $300, $400, $500 an ounce. There were predictions it would reach $2,000, and more. It did not escape my wife's notice that she was suddenly making more profit because gold that had cost her $300 was now $400 and was pushing up the market price of gold jewelry. She thought it might be a good idea to buy a lot more gold than her current needs and profit from its price increases which at that time seemed to have no end. She finally decided to focus her attention on her jewelry instead of being a part time gold speculator. Gold eventually hit $800 and then the bottom fell out. By buying only what she needed, she may have missed a little profit, but she avoided a potentially serious loss.

Some Unexpected Players

It is not only the Hedge Fund operators and other well known Hot Shots that have gotten into big time speculation. A number of old, successful companies have strayed from the main business that has made them successful, and have been tempted by speculative sure things. These ventures have often injured the companies. One example is a large manufacturer. It was a high quality growth company, successful and financially strong. It could have been satisfied with normal business profits as my wife was, but greed and gullibility led them astray. For big potential profits, management ventured into a speculative, highly leveraged operation that has almost ruined the company. In 1989 its net worth was $4.4 billion, by 1993 it had lost 67% of its value and was worth $1.4 billion. The stockholders have been badly hurt. The dividend has been slashed from $1.40 to $.20, an 86% drop. Procter & Gamble's management recently decided to engage in currency futures speculation. The losses did not wound the company seriously, but it was both embarrassing and painful. Perhaps management has gotten the picture and now has a better understanding of the business.

The Lesson

If the sharpest speculators and some of the top level managers of our biggest corporations can get burned, are you far behind? A wise man learns from his experience, a wiser man learns from the experience of others.

CHAPTER 10

Selecting Stocks

The Heart of the Matter

Surely the selection of stocks for your portfolio is the heart of the investment process. Stocks come in all shapes and sizes and, if you are to be successful and comfortable, they must fit your needs. It is my job to devise a method that considers, as best I can, the various factors that are important to you and provide a structure flexible enough to accommodate every need.

Key Factors

These are the factors I considered:

1. SAFETY While there are quite a few investors who are more interested in action than safety, they are traders and speculators. That is not my bag. As a long-term investor, safety is always a top priority with me.

2. PROFIT I said safety is a top priority, profitability is equally important. An unprofitable investment is useless. In fact it is a drain on your portfolio and cannot be tolerated.

3. INCOME This factor may be of little interest to the investors during their working years, but is apt to be very important to a retiree.

4. SIMPLICITY Management of your assets is a very important matter, far too important to be left to hired managers that may have tens of thousands of customers. Whether they have 50 or 50,000, you are only a number to them. All the money they manage is put into one pool, whatever the individual needs or desires of the investors. This saves you time and relieves you of the bother of making decisions. BUT there is a cost, and it is not trivial. You are guaranteed mediocre performance, less expenses. Most investors are unwary and choose this alternative. Their motto is, "Play now. Pay later."

Who is most interested in your future? Not the asset managers! Like you and everyone else, they are interested in their own welfare. If you would tolerate it, they would quickly increase your fees for management. This is a job for you. It will take some thoughtful attention and some of your time. However, I am realistic. Regardless of the future benefits, few people will go for any investment management plan that entails a heavy burden of time and effort. Rather than that, most people would give up and rely on a broker or mutual fund manager. Even so, the plan must be effective and enable you to select and maintain a high quality portfolio.

Value Line -The Happy Medium

I have tried to make the maximum use of logic and common sense. In some cases this has involved discarding ancient traditions and practices that were possibly useful 200 years ago, but are impediments to the modern investor. Investment professionals have generally ignored Admiral Hopper's warning against doing something just because we always did it that way. Notice these departures from conventionality. Don't either accept or reject ideas out of hand. Read my explanation and test it against your own common sense.

Statement of Objectives

So, before starting your selection, it is important to define as accurately as possible why you are saving. Exactly what do you hope this program will accomplish? Until you are able to write a precise statement of your investment objectives, it probably is not clearly settled in your mind. As an example, I shall show you my own statement. This will not fit your needs since your situation will be different than mine, but it will give you an idea. "My investment objective is to produce as much income as is consistent with safety and maintaining moderate growth in both principal and income, well above the inflation rate, and do this without getting mired in bookkeeping, complex research and computations, spending a lot of time or money." There is no mistaking what this means and any purchase that I make, or any change, must serve the purpose of my objective.

Shooting Themselves in the Foot

Unfortunately most retirees think only of maximum current income and ignore the long-term effects of low total return and inflation. This is likely to be a painful error. The worst of it is that, when they begin to feel the pinch, they are already in serious trouble, and they still do not understand that they did it to themselves. When preparing your own objectives, however close or far from retirement, give inflation your most careful attention and be sure your objective is designed to cope with it. A common error when inflation is low is to think it will never again increase. This would make bond and other fixed income securities seem less unsafe. Even should that miracle occur, you know from your study of compounding that even low inflation is serious after a few years.

An Important Step

At first glance you might think that the idea of writing down your objective is a useless drill, but I want to emphasize its very real value. This is not "homework", not a paper to hand in or even to show to anyone else, unless you wish to. This is strictly for your own benefit. Anything you can not define in writing is not firmly fixed in your mind or completely understood. The exercise of writing it and perhaps rewriting will bring it into sharp focus. If you keep your records in a file folder, it is a good idea to paste your statement to the front inside cover. Every time you consider any investment transaction ask yourself, "Is this move consistent with my objectives?" Even if you think the value is marginal, you have embarked on a serious business, and even the slightest help can compound into something important.

The Objectives

With the innumerable combinations of savings and pension plans as well as differing personal situations and preferences, I will not make any effort to personalize a program. My approach will be generic and you can adjust it as required. I will list some approaches that investors might want to consider in preparing their own objectives.

1. Accumulate as large a stake as your income and your personal situation will permit. There is no danger it will be too much.

2. Make certain that no consideration of profit, or anything else, is permitted to compromise the safety of your principal.

3. For some, an objective might be easier to follow if it were more specific, such as a target amount to be accumulated or a target percentage of earnings to commit to the program. For example, investors might wish to accumulate $1,000,000 by the time they are 62, or they might decide to contribute 10% of their gross income to the program. The specificity is appealing, but, to use this method successfully, you should review it frequently, perhaps every three years or so. As time goes on and conditions change, it may become apparent that your original target amount won't accomplish what you intended. This gives you the opportunity to revise it in time to be effective.

Getting the Information

Before you can begin to evaluate stocks for selection, the first step is to figure out where you can get the reliable information you will need. Fortunately, there is ample information available on stocks that are publicly traded, and it is unlikely that you would want to invest in any others. Several companies publish reference material that you can subscribe to. These are quite expensive, however, costing hundreds of dollars per year. Most people prefer to consult them at a public library where they are widely available. From my experience the following are the most popular with investors: Moody's Handbook, Standard & Poors Stock Guide, and the Value Line Investment Survey. They all furnish valuable information you will want and are updated periodically. I recommend that you examine all three to see which seems easiest to use. Of course there is nothing to prevent you from double checking your selection with another authority. All three have their good points and I do not consider any one as clearly superior. For purposes of instruction, however, I think it helpful to use concrete examples of real live companies, and for that purpose I will use Value Line. I won't describe the book at this time except to say that it regularly reports on about 1700 stocks, grouped by industry. A full page is devoted to each company. The information is kept up to date and is well indexed. You will become more familiar with the material as we go along.

First, a Look at Value Line

To get right into the subject, let us start by taking a look at Figure 2, *(next page)* a page from Value Line and see what it looks like. This is the page devoted to the Walgreen Co. There is a great deal of information here, current, historical, and some predictions for the future. You will recognize that there are two very different kinds of information, some of it is actual fact and some is judgment. You can rely on the statistics, the predictions and other matters of judgment should be tested by your own common sense or sometimes with another authority. The hundreds of figures listed comprise just about all the statistical information an investor would want to know. No individual investor could possibly analyze every item of information, weigh its value, and decide how to use it. We are each operating a business. It is very important, but we have other important concerns as well. Time is valuable, and we must consider how much time we can reasonably devote to this business. With this in mind I have streamlined the information we will use. The items I omit are not necessarily useless, but I feel our time can be used more efficiently focusing our efforts on the most important factors. As time goes on and you gain experience, you may wish to add another item or two to your own list.

What Information do we See?

1. The most prominent feature on the page is the graph showing the price performance of the stock for the past decade or so. On this particular chart two things are obvious, the price has steadily increased and the rate of increase has been remarkably consistent. Incidentally, although I do not use it as a formal measurement, I value consistency greatly. One thing that is not evident at first glance is the use of a logarithmic scale. While it is useful in showing relative increase, it flattens out the curve. Unless you look carefully at the figures you would not realize that the price of the shares has increased ten-fold since 1984.

2. Just below the graph there are rows of figures. Lines 1, 3, and 4 show the sales, the earnings, and the dividends per share since 1980. You will note that all of these have increased at about the same rate. You will also notice that each of these figures has increased <u>every</u> year since 1980 with two exceptions, in 1987 earnings were the same as the previous year and the '82 dividend was the same as '81.

3. There are more rows of figures you can examine at leisure, but below them is a narrow box, titled Business, that gives basic information about the company, what it does and what products or services it sells.

Figure 2

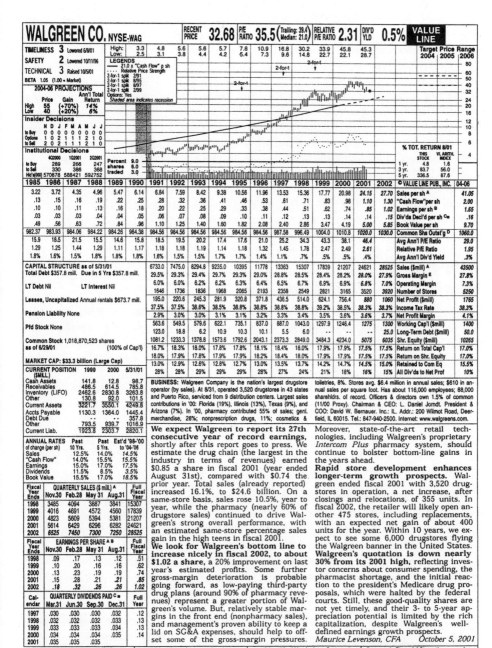

4. Below that is a large narrative section describing current operations and problems including a general assessment of the company's future and its suitability as an investment.

5. Below that on the right is a line showing Value Line's assessment of the company's financial strength. In essence financial strength is the company's ability to overcome economic adversity. The ratings go from C to A++. This company is rated A+.

6. A bit more than halfway down the page, on the left, is a box labeled ANNUAL RATES of change. The Sales and Earnings rates are the most important to the long-term investor. Those already retired will also be interested in dividend increases, but these usually correspond closely with earnings growth. These rates will be of prime importance in our evaluations for investment selection.

7. At the very top of the page is shown the recent price per share, the P/E, or price earnings ratio, and the dividend yield. I will discuss the P/E and its significance as we go along.

8. You may wonder why I have omitted discussion of the Timeliness and Safety ratings so prominently displayed. First, the Timeliness rating considers the next 6 to 12 months and, in my opinion has minimal value for a long-term investor. The safety rating, too, is aimed at the traders and the test we will use in selection will be more appropriate to our purpose.

There are many more items of information, some of which may be of interest, but these are the ones I suggest will be the most useful to you.

How High is Up?

Now you have settled on objectives, and have seen the kind of information that is available about the companies you will eventually buy. Objectives are vital, but knowing that you want maximum growth consistent with safety is difficult to apply directly to a page of information. You need some measurement tools to tell you **how** profitable this company is or **how** safe, and how to choose between companies. The way to do this is to develop numerical standards which will enable you to weed out mediocre or risky investments and narrow your selection to a very few of the best. People will develop their own standards guided by their own objectives and, as time goes on, their experience.

What Kind of Company do we Want?

Since we want our savings to grow, we want to own a company whose earnings will grow. While not the only test, past performance is about the best indicator of future performance. We want a company whose earnings have shown healthy growth. For a double check we also want consistent growth in sales (or revenues) because earnings are dependent on revenues. Equally important is safety of our assets and, while growing earnings and sales are evidence of safety, we must confirm that by checking the financial strength rating. These are the basic points, although we also want to make sure that we are not paying too high a price for these earnings. Now to devise standards that will insure a sound selection.

What Standards?

It will take you a while to develop your own standards, but for the purpose of illustration, following are the ones I use in selecting stocks for my own portfolio. I apply these roughly in order, and as soon as a stock under examination fails **any** standard, I turn the page and do not waste any more time on it. Here are the ones I use:

1. The graph of price performance must trend upward at a good angle and be relatively smooth and consistent. A good looking chart is consistent with earnings and sales growth. It is not proof by itself but is a double check.

2. The financial strength rating must be at least A, preferably A+ or A++. If it is only A, it must score exceptionally high on the other measurements.

3. The annual rate of earnings growth should be in double digits for the past 10 years, the past 5 years, and the estimate for the next 3 to 5 years. If one of those figures were 9% and the rest exceeded my standards, I would leave it on the list for consideration. The rate of dividend growth is usually about the same as the earnings rate.

4. Sales (or revenue) growth is an important check on earnings growth. I am not able to assign an appropriate numerical value, because it varies by industry though it is usually lower than earnings growth. For the stocks you will be considering it may be in the 4-8% range. If it were very low or a negative growth, that would be a danger signal.

5. Setting a P/E standard is troublesome for me. The P/E is the current price of the stock divided by its present annual earnings per share. Clearly, when you are looking at the very best stocks, the P/E is likely to be higher than average. How much higher is it prudent to go? I have seen average P/Es go from more than 20 to less than 10. The P/E is, in effect, a stock's popularity index. It is normally based on a consensus among investors as to a stock's future earnings, considering its past performance and future prospects. Sometimes, however, especially in high tech companies, speculative fever drives the P/E to astronomical levels, perhaps 100 or more and there are many stocks selling for a high price that have no P/E because they are new companies

that have no earnings. You can easily distinguish the solid companies from the speculative, but even a few of the best have quite high P/Es. Selecting good stocks with high valuation is a tricky business and I would advise caution. Until you have a lot of experience it is safer to set a limit of about 1½ times the average P/E. Later in the book I will discuss the problem of high P/Es in more detail.

For a gambler speculation may provide a thrill, but it is no place for a conservative long-term investor. For myself, I begin to look very carefully at even the best companies at one and a half times the average, at present that is about 25. This is no magic number. Investors must decide for themselves.

Danger in High P/E

The reason a company's stock price is disproportionately high compared with its earnings (a high P/E) is that investors believe the company's earnings will soon be much better. More often than not in the case of very high P/E's investors are over optimistic. If a stock has a P/E of 60 and doesn't meet expectations, its P/E may drop to 15, and the stock will quickly lose three quarters of its value. How this works out in real life is illustrated in a recent study which appeared in a David Babson & Co. Staff Letter. A statistical summary of its results is reproduced on the next page.

Figure 3

*Cullinane Database Systems changed its name to Cullinet Software in 1983 and merged into computer Associates in 1989.

#Marion Labs changed its name to Marion Merrell Dow in 1989 when Dow Chemical acquired 67% of Marion's stock.

March	Name	Top P/E ratio NYSE	S & P 500 P/E ratio	Change in value of stock to 4/93	Change in value S&P 500 to 4/93
1982	NBI	24	7	-99%	+298%
1983	Culinane*	44	12	-28%	+128%
1984	Advanced Micro	35	11	unchanged	+180
1985	Cullinet*1	37	11	-20%	+146
1986	Marion Labs #	53	15	+13	+87
1987	Marion Labs#	68	17	-47	+53
1988	Rollins Environ'l	34	14	-58	+72
1989	Century Tel	29	13	+28	+51
1990	Total Systems	47	14	+8	+31
1991	U.S. Surgical	63	15	-45	+19
1992	U.S. Surgical	70	15	-73	+10

© David Babson Co.

Obviously no one who bought any of these stocks used any standards similar to the ones I have discussed. Whatever criteria they used, I wouldn't recommend. It was probably impulse or "seat of the pants" investing. Of the 11 listings, only three went up in price, and those three did poorly compared with the market. The others all lost, some lost heavily. The average person never hears about the sober and careful investing you will do, but this kind of speculation is high profile and makes many people think all investing in stocks is equally dangerous.

6. The yield is more important to the retiree than to those saving for retirement. Most investors like a dividend, whether they need it or not. A dividend does reduce price volatility, but this does not affect long term performance. One thing does matter, however. You pay taxes on dividends and, if you reinvest them, you pay a commission. Earnings that the company retains are immediately reinvested in the business - no tax, no commission. You do not get extra shares, but this helps to increase share value.

7. The last step is most important. Read the description of the company's business and the narrative. Is this a company you would be comfortable owning? Have you enough confidence in its future that you could tolerate a crash like October 1987 without panicking and selling out at a loss? If yes, it belongs on your list for further consideration.

Evaluating Company Management?

All investment professionals stress the importance of management, which is obviously vital. They talk to company officials, inspect plants and make their judgments about management before buying or recommending the stock. You and I are not big wheels. We have no access to the people who manage large corporations. Do we then have to go to some professional and pay a fee to get his or her opinion? Luckily, this is not necessary. For a company just starting out, or unproved, or in trouble, a close examination of its management would be important, but we are not going to be looking at such companies anyway. For the companies we are considering, our criteria will be, in effect, management's report card. We'll be considering the cream of the crop. This status was not achieved by poor management. It would be like asking Joe DiMaggio to prove that he had adequate training to qualify as a big league ballplayer.

No Exceptions

These will be your own standards. They will not be imposed on you by anyone else, but you should apply them in a disciplined way. Once you have considered carefully and decided on your investment rules **NEVER** make any exceptions. You may well find as you gain experience that you want to make adjustments. Do not hesitate once you have carefully considered. Then apply the new standards strictly. I know that "never" is a long time, and I suppose that an experienced investor will want to make a minor exception or two. Still, unless you want to modify your rules to permit the action as a regular procedure, you ought not to deviate. Self discipline is tough to maintain, but you should try hard to do it. These are the rules that represent your own best business judgment. If you let down the bars you may wind up with an untidy portfolio that is unlikely to achieve your objectives.

Going through the Steps

Now let's take another look at Walgreen, Figure 4, *(page 75)* and go through the steps as if we were considering buying it.

1. The first thing to look at is the graph at the top of the page showing the price performance of the shares for the past 10 or 15 years. It shows a steady upward trend with the expectable interruption of the Crash of '87. It immediately resumed its climb, and the curve is close to a straight line. It is certainly going up, but will the increase measure up to our requirements? We can see that the stock price in 1984, adjusted for subsequent splits, was about $4. In 12 years it has increased 10 fold, which is very good indeed.

2. Next is our check for safety. Looking at the financial strength rating at the lower right hand corner of the page, we find it rated A+, a very good rating that meets my own requirements. This rating, however, is not an actual fact, but a matter of judgment. While I do not question this rating, safety is so important that I sometimes double check it with Standard & Poors. In this case, as usual, the S&P rating of A+ confirms Value Line. The S&P ratings can be found in the S&P Stock Guide in the library or from your broker.

3. Now we go to the middle of the left edge of the page, to the box labeled ANNUAL RATES.

a. The sales increases, well into the double digits are exceptionally high - a very healthy sign.

b. Earnings increases, the most important measurement of all, are excellent, slightly higher than sales and well over my required level.

c. For the retirees, the dividends, as usual, follow the earnings closely. Although the yield at 1.3% looks low, the investors who paid $4 per share are now getting an 11% yield on their cost, and it has increased every year since then.

4. The next place to go is the middle of the top of the page to look at the P/E. This 23.1 is compared with an average of 16.4 for the whole market. That is about 41% above the average. Is this stock worth this premium? Will its future earnings growth justify a P/E of 23.1. While this valuation approaches my resistance point, I feel that the stock's high quality is adequate justification.

5. We have already examined the dividend rate.

6. Having met all the screening tests, it is time to get a feel for the type of industry and the type of company you are considering. You will probably be like me and have a prejudice for or against some industries. Do not worry about it. There are many industry groups and it is better not to own anything that will make you uneasy. And of course there are some industries where there is not a single company that will meet my standards. For example no electric utility maintains double digit earnings growth. Or you may be prejudiced against particular products, perhaps liquor, chewing tobacco, or cigarettes. I am sure the narrative will give you enough information for a sound decision. If you would be comfortable owning it, put it on your list for consideration. I like Walgreen, but others may not.

Figure 4

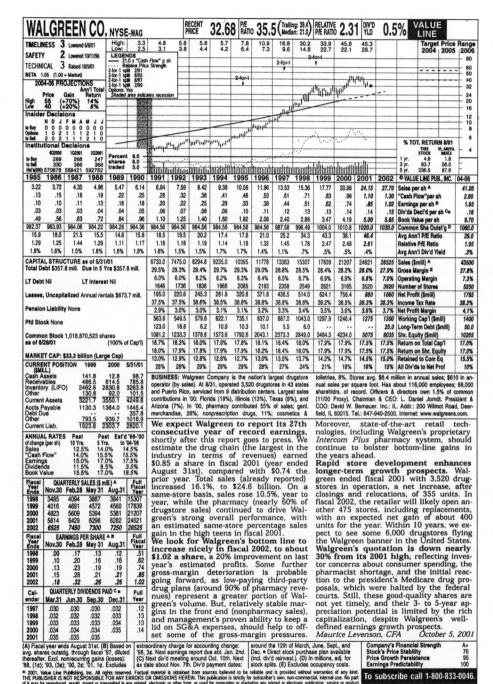

Are Standards Really Necessary?

They certainly are! The use of high standards, strictly applied, makes the difference between businesslike operation and hit or miss. Have you ever watched a pilot preparing to take off? He is well trained, experienced, and has done this a thousand times. He could do it with his eyes closed. But instead he has a checklist, his standards. He follows item by item until he has gone through the whole list. This check helps to ensure a safe and uneventful take off. Your life is not at stake every time you buy or sell a stock, but management of your assets is a very serious business. Even with rigorous standards not every stock will perform up to expectations, but the regular application of standards will sharply reduce the percentage of disappointments. The reason for standards and my insistence on strict self-discipline is simple, but it may surprise you. It protects you against - YOURSELF. We all have weak moments when we want to give in to an impulse. I have them as often as you do. If we have a safety net, we are apt to think twice. Bear in mind that you are not using a formula to select your portfolio. The purpose of the formula is to exclude the unworthy. What you have is a list of top-notch candidates from which to select.

A Common Failure

I am convinced that very few individual investors have any systematic way of measuring and rating stocks as suitable investments. One objection sometimes raised to the use of rigid standards is that they may rule out a stock that will do well. That is absolutely true. But any stock, no matter how miserable, might possibly do well someday. If you do not draw a line with strict standards, selection would be unmanageable. You would have a 1700 stock grab bag. I have rejected quite a few of those in the past 60 years, but I have also rejected many more that turned sour. No selection method is infallible. No one can invariably predict a company's future but the idea of standards is to improve the odds. Instead of buying a company that **might** do well, you want the one that will almost certainly **do** well. This is like a criminal trial in reverse. Instead of having to prove a stock is unsuitable, it is your job to select those that, beyond a reasonable doubt, are suitable. You will surely pass up some good performers, but you will also avoid all of the dogs. If the standards are sound, a stock that meets them is more likely to succeed than one that doesn't. Always keep the odds in your favor. This is where we apply the principle of managing RISK. If a stock's chance of success is 5 to 1, that sounds good, unless you have an alternative whose chances are 20 to 1. You do not want just good odds, you want the best. The ability to understand and apply this principle is one of the tests that separates the sheep from the goats.

The Theory is Plausible. How about the Real World?

I think the best way to illustrate how this method works in practice is to tell a story. This is a story of how my wife, Flash, a goldsmith, saved and invested her earnings. It will be illustrated with a series of photocopies of the actual statements I gave her at the time.

The Thrifty Craftsman

Flash plied her craft for 25 years and during that entire time was saving the profits for the benefit of our grandchildren. Having lived through hard times in the Great Depression, she knew what to do with savings, put it in the bank. My ideas were a lot different. As I suggested in the chapter on Horsepower, I like to see my savings working as hard as I did to earn them. Accordingly, I recommended that she invest her surplus cash in the stock market. She was a bit reluctant and had visions of her hard earned savings being wiped out in some market catastrophe. Eventually she agreed, and I managed the portfolio, small at first. She was still skittish about the market and followed it closely. By October of 1987 she believed stock prices were too high and too volatile and insisted on selling out. I disapproved but the best alternative was to put the proceeds in Treasury bonds, at least for the time being.

The Crash of '87

In about 10 days her hunch paid off when stock prices plunged 25% on October 19th. Flash instantly changed her spots, recognizing a bargain sale. The next day, October 20th, she sold her bonds with a nice profit of about $3,000, since the crash had pushed up their prices, and bought back in. As some will remember, and others can visualize, October 20th was a very busy day. Most people could not even get through to their brokers. Luckily, I could. We wanted to get in at the bottom and came pretty close although executions were so delayed that our last call from the broker was at 9:30 PM. When the day was over she had invested about half and still held on to the other half looking for bargains. She finally wound up with a portfolio bought at about a 20% discount. This meant that when the market recovered she would have a profit of about $25,000, including the bond profit. Figure 5 is a printout of the status of her portfolio at the close of business on October 30th. Notice that in 10 days the stocks she had bought had already increased in value by more than $7,000. Following her portfolio from that time to her retirement in January 1993 will show the result of careful management.

Figure 5

Number Shares	Asset Name	Date Purch	NYSEa Purch	Cost / Share	Total cost	Curr Price	Curr Value	Curr Div	Total Income	Curr Yld	Curr P/E	Total Gain	Month Held	% Invest	Invest Gain	% NYSE Gain	Total Return
200	Amer H Produc	10/20/87	145	68.230	13646	71.000	14200	3.34	668	4.7	12.2	554	0	11.4	4	-3	324
500	BellSouth	10/20/87	145	33.682	16841	40.000	20000	2.20	1100	5.5	11.4	3159	0	16.1	19	-3	14864
200	General Electr	10/20/87	145	45.230	9,046	47.375	9,475	1.40	280	3	14.1	429	0	7.6	5	-3	433
400	Heinz	10/20/87	145	40.115	16,046	41.750	16,700	1.24	496	3	14.6	654	0	13.4	4	-3	324
10,000	Champ	1/1/86	130	1.000	10,000	1.237	12,372	0.11	1,100	8.9	11.2	2,372	22	9.9	24	8	2
51,717	Cash	10/28/87	180.54	1.000	51,717	1	51,717	0.07	3,362	6.5	15.4	0	0	41.6	0	-22	7
Totals		10/31/90			117296		124464		7006	5.6		7168		100	6		

Will it Work a Second Time?

Figure 6 shows the same portfolio in July 1990, two and a half years later. Of the four stocks she bought in October of '87, she still held three. In two and a half years one had a gain of 49%, another 58%, and the third 75%. The assets have also been swelled by additional investment from her business. Aside from her business profits, however, the stocks have appreciated by $58,845 - better than leaving it in the bank. Especially significant is the total return of the stocks from 14% to 47%. Also, as in the previous statement, there is not a single stock showing a loss. These fat profits made Flash nervous again in August '90 and again she sold almost everything, contrary to my advice. This time I was right. The market kept going up. After waiting a couple of months for the crash, she bought back in on October 26, 1990.

Figure 6

July, 1990

Number Shares	Asset Name	Date Purch	NYSEa Purch	Cost / Share	Total cost	Curr Price	Curr Value	Curr Div	Total Income	Curr Yld	Curr P/E	Total Gain	Month Held	% Invest	Invest Gain	% NYSE Gain	Total Return
400	Amer H Produc	10/20/87	145	34.115	13646	50.750	20,300	2.15	860	4.2	13.5	6,654	33	9.1	49	34	20
700	AT&T	3/1/88	150.46	29.422	20,595	37.000	25,900	1.32	924	3.6	13.7	5,305	29	11.6	26	29	14
500	Deluxe C	4/28/88	148.21	23.807	11,904	34.500	17,250	1.04	520	3	18	5,347	27	7.8	45	31	21
300	RR Donnely	11/13/87	138	31.203	9,361	44.375	13,313	0.96	288	2.2	14.6	3,952	33	6	42	41	16
200	General Electr	10/20/87	145	45.230	9,046	71.625	14,325	1.88	376	2.6	15.1	5,279	33	6.4	58	34	21
800	Hanson	8/2/89	192	19.033	15,226	21.000	16,800	1.10	880	5.2	10.5	1,574	12	7.6	10	1	16
800	Heinz	10/20/87	145	20.058	16,046	35.125	28,100	0.84	672	2.4	17.8	12,054	33	12.6	75	34	25
200	Marsh & McG	11/16/87	145	53.480	10,696	74.875	14,975	2.60	520.00	3.5	17.7	4,279	33	6.7	40	41	17
200	Merck	5/2/89	172	67.605	13,521	89.125	17,825	1.80	360.00	2	21.3	4,304	15	8	32	13	27
450	Philip Morr	1/17/90	186.86	39.311	17,690	47.875	21,544	1.38	621.00	2.9	14.6	3,854	6	9.7	22	4	47
200	Royal D	11/7/87	140	52.150	10,430	83.375	16,675	3.50	700.00	4.2	16.5	6,245	33	7.5	60	39	23
10,000	Bank	7/30/90	195	1.000	10,000	1.237	10,000	0.11	499	8.9	11.2	0	22	9.9	24	8	2
5,363	FIDO	7/30/90	195	1.000	5,363	1	5,363	0.07	375	7	14.3	0	0	0	7		
Totals					163524		222370		7595	3.4		58847		100	36		

Yield on the Basis of the original cost = 4.6%

Figure 7 (*next page*) shows the status of the portfolio 3 months later at the end of October. This is the first statement showing any paper losses, but these are all stocks held less than a week. The final illustration, Figure 8, is dated December 31, 1992 at the time she retired, just before the account was liquidated. Again the portfolio contains no losers and the appreciation is almost $100,000 and the annual income is nearly $9,000. In just over 5 years the value of the portfolio had virtually tripled. Much of the increase is attributable to profits from the business that were regularly invested, but the investment profit was very substantial.

A Capitalist

When I was married 58 years ago, I was making $50 a week. As was the custom in the olden days, my wife quit her job and then had an allowance of $10 a week for food and household supplies. With the surplus she bought her clothes. She gradually assumed more responsibilities, and a larger allowance, until she paid almost all the household bills. Some of these charges were paid daily, like food, others monthly or annually. To make sure that she would always have the money to pay when due, she used accrual accounting. If an insurance policy cost $600 a year, she would deposit in advance $50 each month in a bank account and the same for all her other expenses. This was before the convenience of credit cards, but of course the bank was paying us interest instead of us paying them. As our life style improved her bank balance became unreasonably high, and I persuaded her to entrust it to me for investment and you see the result in Figure 8. She now can not decide whether she is a thrifty housewife with savings or a capitalist who pays household bills as a sideline.

Figure 7

October 31, 1990

Number Shares	Asset Name	Date Purch	NYSEa Purch	Cost / Share	Total cost	Curr Price	Curr Value	Curr Div	Total Income	Curr Yld	Curr P/E	Total Gain	Month Held	% Invest	Invest Gain	% NYSE Gain	Total Return
300	Amer H Produc	10/26/90	162.2	48.578	14,573	49.125	14,738	2.15	645	4.4	12.8	164	0	7.8	1	2	128
275	Autodat	10/26/90	162.2	50.583	13,910	50.275	13,826	0.70	193	1.4	15.9	-85	0	7.3	-1	2	-34
1,000	First Ame	10/26/90	162.2	17.876	17,876	16.500	16,500	1.25	1,250	7.6	5.2	-1,376	0	8.7	-8	2	-92
275	General Electr	10/26/90	162.2	50.958	14,013	52.000	14,300	2.06	567	4	10.2	287	0	7.6	2	2	333
750	Hanson	10/26/90	162.2	18.418	13,813	18.125	13,594	1.37	1,028	7.6	7.8	-220	0	7.2	-2	2	-61
425	Heinz	10/26/90	162.2	32.813	13,946	32.250	13,706	0.96	408	3	15	-239	0	7.3	-2	2	-68
500	Lawson	10/26/90	162.2	26.182	13,091	25.500	12,750	0.40	200.00	1.6	12.9	-341	0	6.8	-3	2	-83
450	Philip Morr	1/17/90	186.86	39.311	17,690	47.125	21,206	1.72	774.00	3.6	14.4	3,516	9	11.2	20	-11	29
200	Royal D	11/7/87	140	52.150	10,430	77.625	15,525	4.25	850.00	5.5	15.4	5,095	36	8.2	49	19	20
675	ServiceMaster	10/26/90	162.2	20.799	14,039	20.500	13,838	1.88	1269.00	9.2	9	-202	0	7.3	-1	2	-56
13,712	Bank	7/30/90	166	1.000	13,712	1.000	13,712	0.05	684	5	20	0	0	7.3	0	0	5
5,431	FIDO	10/30/90	166	1.000	5,431	1.000	5,431	0.07	380	7	14.3	0	0	2.9	0	0	7
19,729	Galaxy	10/30/90	166	1.000	19,729	1.000	19,729	0.08	1,513	7	13	0	0	10.4	0	0	8
Totals					182253		188855		9761	5.2		6599		100	4		

Yield on the Basis of the original cost = 5.4%

Figure 8

12/31/92

•Number Shares	Asset Name	Date Purch	NYSEa Purch	Cost/Share	Total cost	Curr Price	Curr Value	Curr Div	Total Income	Curr Yld	Curr P/E	Total Gain	Month Held	% Invest	Invest Gain	% NYSE Gain	Total NYSE Return
500	Abbott	11/20/90	172.48	21.360	10,600	30.750	15,188	0.60	300	2	20.3	4,508	25	4.4	42	19	20
500	Abbott	8/19/91	207	26.290	13,147	30.750	15,188	0.60	300	2	20.3	2,041	16	4.4	16	16	13
20	Abbott	10/6/92	228	29.330	587	30.750	608	0.60	12	2	20.3	21	3	0.2	4	5	18
300	Amer H Produc	10/26/90	162.2	48.578	14,573	67.500	20,250	2.84	852	4.2	13.3	5,677	26	5.8	39	48	20
100	Amer H Produc	4/23/91	204	61.050	6,105	67.500	6,750	2.84	284	4.2	13.3	645	20	1.9	11	18	10
150	Amer H Produc	5/28/91	205	61.130	9,170	67.500	10,125	2.84	426	4.2	13.3	956	19	2.9	10	17	11
20	Amer H Produc	10/6/92	228	66.575	1,332	67.500	1,350	2.84	57	4.2	13.3	19	3	0.4	1	5	10
550	Autodat	10/26/90	162.2	25.292	13,911	53.125	29,219	0.46	253	0.9	26.2	15,308	26	8.4	110	48	41
550	Autodat	8/19/91	207	31.730	6,346	53.125	10,625	0.46	92	0.9	26.2	4,279	16	3.1	67	16	47
300	Deluxe	11/20/90	172.48	33.328	9,998	46.750	14,025	1.40	420	3	19	4,027	25	4	40	39	20
300	Deluxe	10/23/91	214	40.992	12,298	46.750	14,025	1.40	420	3	19	1,727	14	4	14	12	15
1,000	Fst Ame	10/25/90	163.3	17.876	17,876	38.875	38,875	1.40	1,400	3.7	11.9	19,999	26	10.9	112	48	45
20	Fst Ame	10/5/92	228	33.950	679	38.875	758	1.40	28	3.7	11.9	79	2	0.2	12	5	4
275	General Electr	10/25/90	162	50.958	14,013	85.500	23,513	2.52	693	2.9	14.9	9,499	26	6.8	68	48	30
200	General Electr	5/28/91	205	73.860	12,926	85.500	14,963	2.52	441	2.9	14.9	2,037	19	4.3	16	17	13
480	GL Chem	12/21/92	237	68.340	32,803	69.250	33,240	0.32	154	0.5	19.6	437	0	9.6	1	1	61
425	Heinz	10/26/90	162.2	32.813	13,946	44.125	18,753	1.20	510	2.7	17.7	4,808	26	5.4	34	48	17
25	Heinz	10/6/92	228	40.335	1,008	44.125	1,003	1.20	30	2.7	17.7	95	3	0.3	9	5	49
450	Philip Morr	1/17/90	186.86	39.311	17,690	77.125	34,706	2.60	1,170	3.4	13.3	17,016	35	10	96	29	29
100	Philip Morr	4/23/91	204	68.050	6,805	77.125	7,713	2.60	260	3.4	13.3	907	20	2.2	13	18	11
50	Philip Morr	5/28/91	205	69.330	3,467	77.125	3,856	2.60	130	3.4	13.3	390	19	1-Jan	11	17	10
300	Walgreen	6/8/92	228	31.670	9,485	43.125	12,938	0.60	180	1.4	22.5	3,452	7	3.7	3.7	36	5
300	Walgreen	8/25/92	226	38.970	11,691	43.125	12,938	0.60	180	1.4	22.5	1,247	4	3.7	11	6	35
5,000	Bank	12/29/92	240	1.000	5,000	1.000	5,000	0.03	125	2.5	40	0	0	1.4	0	0	3
2,000	Galaxy	12/29/92	240	1.000	2,000	1	2,000	0.03	56	2.8	35.7	0	0	0.6	0	0	3
Totals					247,456		347,609		8,773	2.5		99,174		100	40		

Yield on the Basis of the original cost = 3.5%

Butterfly or Philosopher?

My wife has the same problem as an ancient Chinese philosopher. Every night he dreamed he was a butterfly. After 40 or 50 years, his dream world was just as real to him as his other world. He was unable to decide whether he was a philosopher dreaming he was a butterfly or a butterfly dreaming he was a philosopher.

My own Portfolio

Figure 9 is my own present portfolio, warts and all. The only change I have made is in the number of shares. This is far from a model portfolio, but in the real world I have never seen one. Uneven growth, capital gains liability, need for income, etc. make a live portfolio a lot different from a classroom model. It does have some good points. It has been very profitable. Look at the total return. But everything has been profitable lately. True enough, but look at a couple of columns of the printout near the right edge, showing the % gain for each lot and the next column showing the same for the NYSE for the same period. My gain is one and a half to twice that of the market, and more.

Figure 9

11/29/96

•Number Shares	Asset Name	Date Purch	NYSEa Purch	Cost / Share	Total cost	Curr Price	Curr Value	Curr Div	Total Income	Curr Yld	Curr P/E	Total Gain	Month Held	% Invest	Invest Gain	% NYSE Gain	Total Return
400	Autodat	7/13/94	252	26.639	10656	42.875	17,150	0.46	184	1.1	33.8	6,494	29	9.6	61	58	23.2
275	Campbell	7/13/94	252	35.998	9,899	82.625	22,722	1.54	424	1.9	31.6	12,822	29	12.7	130	58	43.7
300	General Electr	5/28/91	205	36.935	11,081	104.000	31,200	1.84	552	1.8	32	20,120	66	17.4	182	94	22.5
238	HWP	1/9/96	330	39.793	9,471	53.875	12,822	0.48	114	0.9	20.3	3,352	11	7.2	35	21	41.5
300	Merck	11/20/90	172.48	28.630	8,581	83.000	24,900	1.60	480.00	0.1	34.2	16,319	72	13.9	190	131	21.3
160	Microsoft	7/15/96	339.67	56.416	9,027	81.750	13,080	0.00	0	0.0	42.1	4,053	4	7	45	18	N/A
107	Proctor Gam	1/9/96	330	87.874	9,403	108.750	11,636	1.80	193.00	1.7	25.2	2,234	11	6.5	24	21	28.8
200	Schering P	1/9/95	251	37.139	7,428	71.250	14,250	1.32	264.00	1.9	27.8	6,822	23	8	92	59	43
1,045	SvcMaster	5/28/91	205	8.948	9,351	25.750	26,909	0.68	711	2.6	16.8	17,558	66	15	188	94	23.8
4,435	Cash	11/29/96	398	1.000	4,435	1	4,435	0.05	222	5.0	20	0	0	2.5	0	0	N/A
Totals					89,332		179,104		3,144	2		89,774		100	100		

Yield on the Basis of the original cost = 3.5%

11/29/96   FIGURE 9

Is it Transferable?

You may be convinced that I know how to invest profitably, but does it follow that I can teach it to you? Will the method shown in the book give the same results? These are reasonable and important questions and I think I can give you a good answer. But in order to make it work the reader must contribute two ingredients. The first is normal intelligence, but the second is a lot harder - motivation. Most investors are addicted to a half-baked approach. They rely on a broker or mutual funds or other advice. If a person understands the problem and is determined to do it right, this will work fine, otherwise it will not help much.

The Bishop's Dilemma

A couple of years ago my good friend Tom Ray, the Episcopal Bishop of Northern Michigan, came to me with a problem. He was dissatisfied with the performance of the diocesan endowment fund. Normally I would expect that investment and return would be managed by the broker and the bank that were paid to do that job under the supervision of the trust association. But when the income was progressively less adequate to serve the needs of the Diocese, the bishop had to intervene personally. He came to see me with the printouts of all the investments, but before we looked at them he explained his problem. "The thing that puzzles me," he said, "is that although our investments are doing very well, having doubled in value in the past 15 years, the income is less adequate each year."

The Sharp Horns

My first thought was to check the Consumer Price Index. After looking at that I said, "Tom, while your investment's dollar value was doubling, the value of the dollar has decreased 60%. The real value of the portfolio is now only 80% of what it was 15 years ago." He was stunned, and I asked whether the broker or bank trust officer explained what was happening. No, both said it was doing very well. We then looked at the investments. I already knew what I was going to see, lots of bonds and utilities - low growth, low earnings, high yield. The bishop's dilemma had two sharp horns. The earnings were low and the growth even slower. If he kept the high-income securities, the portfolio would dwindle away, but if he replaced them with good long term investments he would suffer an immediate sharp loss of income that would take 5 years at least to heal.

What to do?

The bishop borrowed an early draft of this book. After reading it he asked and got permission to make copies for the members of the Diocesan Trust Association. Soon after, the bishop sent me the note shown in Figure 10. Several weeks ago the bishop called me and said that a year and a half ago the trust sold 2 million dollars worth of bonds and slow growing securities and replaced them with the kind of stocks I recommend. These are now worth more than $3 million.

Figure 10

Ken Hogg's book has transformed the strategy of the board members of the Trust Association of the Episcopal Diocese of Northern Michigan. We now have a clear criteria and discipline for buying or selling equities. In the past we had a "balanced portfolio" which was relentlessly eroded by inflation and often took capital gains in the performing stocks while keeping the underperforming. As one member said, "Tom, it is scary when I think back on how we made decisions ten years ago."

The Rt. Rev. Thomas K. Ray, Bishop
The Diocese of Northern Michigan

Are Standards Worth the Trouble?

I think this is a good record, and I think the result was well worth the trouble. The portfolio was well managed, but clearly there was another favorable factor at work. We all know that the market as a whole was doing very well. The average investor that relied on hunches, tips from friends, and advice from brokers would have made a profit. He or she might have achieved an annual return of 10, 11, or even 12 percent. If you look at the total return in figure 11, (*next page*) especially the older and larger holdings, that probably average twice that. These results and particularly their consistency can not be just a coincidence.

Figure 11

Number Shares	Asset Name	Date Purch	12/12/96 NYSEa Cost/Share Purch	Total cost	Curr Price	Curr Value	Curr Div	Total Income	Curr Yld	Curr P/E	Total Gain	Month Held	% Invest	Invest Gain	% NYSE Gain	Total Return
4,000	Amer H P	1/22/81	76 / 7.351	29,404	61.250	245,000	1.64	6,560	2.7	21.3	215,596	191	15.4	733	404	17
1,000	Amer H P	3/18/93	240 / 31.095	31,095	61.250	61,250	1.64	1,640	2.7	21.3	30,155	45	3.9	97	60	22.6
500	Campbell	1/21/94	251 / 45.730	22,857	80.375	40,188	1.54	770	1.9	23.6	17,331	25	2.5	76	53	33.5
1,300	Campbell	1/8/96	330 / 58.491	76,038	80.375	104,488	1.54	2,002	1.9	23.6	28,449	11	6.6	37	16	42.8
2,000	Fst Am B	3/8/91	204 / 24.830	49,660	55.750	111,500	1.88	3,760	3.4	13.1	61,840	69	7	125	88	18.4
1,600	General EI	5/24/93	248 / 46.517	74,427	96.750	154,800	1.84	2,944	1.9	21.3	80,373	43	9.8	108	55	24.8
200	General EI	9/13/95	310 / 60.653	12,131	96.750	19,350	1.84	368	1.9	21.3	7,219	15	1.2	60	55	47.3
200	Hewlet P	11/22/95	319 / 42.820	8,564	50.875	10,175	0.48	96	0.9	19.1	1,611	13	0.6	19	20	18.7
650	Hewlet P	12/18/95	331 / 39.181	25,468	50.875	33,069	0.48	312	0.9	19.1	7,601	12	2.1	30	16	31.4
200	Hewlet P	2/29/96	359 / 51.068	10,214	50.875	10,175	0.48	96	0.9	19.1	-39	9	0.6	0	7	0.5
425	JP	6/7/96	363 / 51.596	21,928	57.000	24,225	1.44	612	2.5	12.8	2,297	6	1.5	10	6	23.9
775	McD	11/21/94	251 / 29.663	22,989	45.625	35,359	0.30	233	0.7	19.8	12,371	25	2.2	54	53	23.9
2,700	Merck	4/20/89	171 / 22.505	60,763	76.250	205,875	1.60	4,320	2.1	23.8	145,112	92	13	239	124	19.4
600	Merck	7/10/89	180 / 23.660	14,196	76.250	45,750	1.60	960	2.1	23.8	31,554	89	2.9	222	113	19.2
160	Microsoft	7/15/96	338 / 56.516	9,043	81.000	12,960	0.00	0	0	41.8	3,917	5	0.8	43	13	*
440	Microsoft	8/6/96	352 / 60.929	26,809	81.000	35,640	0.00	0	0	41.8	8,831	4	2.2	33	9	*
6,750	SvcMastr	3/1/90	183 / 6.507	43,922	25.125	169,594	0.68	4,590	2.7	14.6	125,672	81	10.7	286	109	?
3,150	SvcMastr	3/18/93	240 / 13.047	41,098	25.125	79,144	0.68	2,142	2.7	14.6	38,046	45	5	93	60	21.9
2,400	Walgreen	6/9/92	228 / 15.743	37,783	39.375	94,500	0.48	1,152	1.2	24.6	56,717	54	6	150	69	23.8
1,500	Walgreen	9/13/95	310 / 26.726	40,089	39.375	59,063	0.48	720	1.2	24.6	18,974	15	3.7	47	24	37.7
32,000	Bank	12/11/96	384 / 1.000	32,000	1.000	32,000	0.04	1,344	4.2	23.8	0	0	2	0	0	*
173	MM1	12/11/96	384 / 1.000	173	1	173	0.04	7	4.2	23.8	0	0	0	0	0	*
2,114	MM2	12/11/96	384 / 1.000	2,114	1.000	2,114	0.04	89	4.2	23.8	0	0	0.1	0	0	*
Totals				692,765		1,586,392		34,717	3.4		893,627		100	36		

Yield on the Basis of the original cost = 5%

* Total return is more reliable the longer a stock is held. Until a stock has been held for 6 months it is of little value

Making the List

You will not just automatically zero in on a stock to select, you will have some kind of list. You may not want to follow my example, but every six months or so I go through the entire Value Line Survey's 1700 stocks applying my standards, and that process weeds out all but about 75 to 100 stocks, the cream of the crop. The rest of the weeding is by comparison and judgment, and maybe a little prejudice. You have to use some kind of process to make your final selection, but the method you use at this point will make less difference than you would think because <u>all</u> the companies on the list are exceptional, the only way you could go really wrong would be failure to diversify between industries. Sometimes you have to pass up some very good companies because there are better ones in the same industry. This seems like a massive undertaking, but it is a lot easier than it sounds. Here is how I do it. Starting at the front of the book, I look at the first page, 103, and look at the lower right hand corner for the financial strength. If lower than A, I flip over to the next page and keep searching until I find an A or better. When I find one that passes, I look at the annual rates and if earnings are not in double digits, I turn the page. If they are in double digits, I list it and the page number because I will come back to it. And, in the same way, I go through the whole book. I then have about 100 listings but I have not made the complete check. I then make my first check. There are some companies or industries I do not like or do not understand and I cross these out. I then go back to my list and review the page for each stock step by step. I am stricter on the ones rated only A. Unless they are exceptional in the other measurements, I cross them out. Those that pass the test are prime candidates for selection.

You will save this list for making future selections as well. My purpose in checking it periodically is to keep up to date. If I need to make a change I am in a better position to act promptly. Every time I go through the book, I find one or two companies I have never heard of.

Examples of those that Do not Measure Up

The process of selection is, in a sense, just the reverse. You select the good companies by weeding out the bad. It is like panning for gold. At the start your pan has a lot of sand and gravel with a few flakes of heavier gold. When you have gradually washed away the lighter waste material, what's left is (almost) pure gold. I have picked three examples that illustrate how these standards are applied and the kinds of decisions you will have to make. Figure 12 *(next page)* shows the page of Forest Oil Corp. Just looking at the chart of price performance should convince prudent long-term investors that this stock is unsuitable for their portfolios. There is no real need to look further, but, if you do, you will find it passes none of our tests. This company may eventually turn around and do well, but it is not a good prospect for a conservative investor.

Figure 12

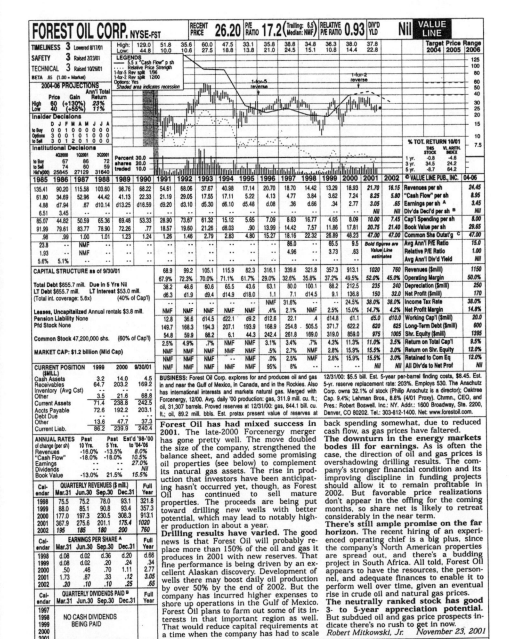

A Goat in Sheep's Clothing

Now look at Consolidated Edison. Figure 13 *(next pages)* shows how it looked to Value Line in March of '93. Here is what I wrote about it at that time, "This is a high grade Electric Utility. . . . It is a general and logical rule that over any extended period the price of a stock (and usually its dividends) will advance at about the same rate as its earnings . . . . When we look at the price performance of Con Edison's stock, we notice an amazing thing. For the past dozen years the price of the stock has been increasing at about 12.8%. . . . (while) the rate of earnings increase for the same period has been about 3.7% and has been declining. What unusual circumstance would account for this discrepancy? Well, dividends have been increasing by 8% per year, well over twice as fast as earnings. While the company may have sound reasons for increasing dividends at an 8% rate, this happy ride will soon come to a screeching halt." Stay tuned.

How did it work out?

The story continues in Figure 14 *(next pages)*. About 6 months after I wrote the above, the stock's price started to drop. The dividend growth rate had been declining steadily and by 1996 it had shrunk to 2% from the 10% of the preceding decade. The income growth is less than inflation, and with declining stock price, stockholders may well be uncomfortable. Like all other electric utilities, this is no place for a conservative investor.

A Very Different Situation

The last company I have is Figure 15 *(next pages)* and it is not a horrible example. Jefferson Pilot is a life insurance company. The only faint cloud on the horizon is the financial strength rating just A, the lowest I would consider. But growth in revenues, earnings, dividends, and stock price are all very good, the P/E is very low, and the narrative is encouraging. It also has a yield that a retiree can appreciate. I think it is undervalued and I recently added it to my own portfolio.

Figure 13

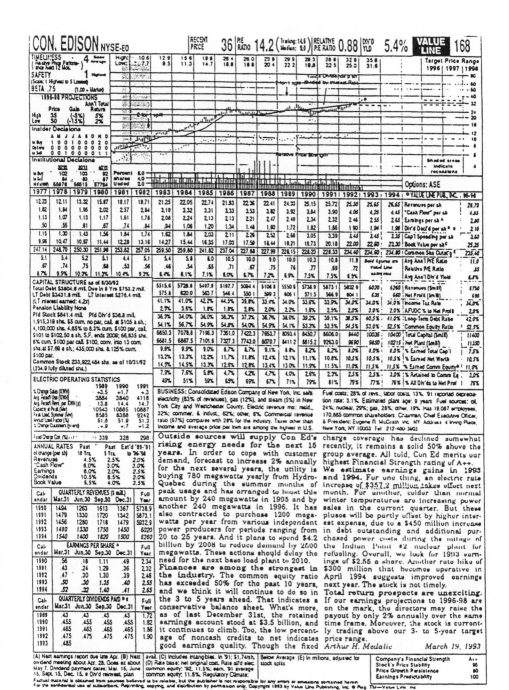

Figure 14

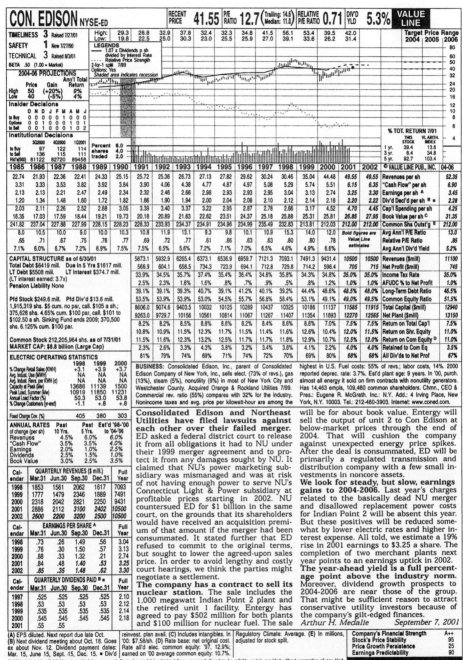

Value Line report for CON. EDISON NYSE-ED

RECENT PRICE **41.55** | P/E RATIO **12.7** (Trailing: 14.6 / Median: 11.0) | RELATIVE P/E RATIO **0.71** | DIV'D YLD **5.3%** | **VALUE LINE**

TIMELINESS **3** Raised 7/27/01
SAFETY **1** New 7/27/90
TECHNICAL **3** Raised 8/3/01
BETA .50 (1.00 = Market)

BUSINESS: Consolidated Edison, Inc., parent of Consolidated Edison Company of New York, Inc., sells elect. (73% of revs.), gas (13%), steam (5%), nonutility (9%) in most of New York City and Westchester County. Acquired Orange & Rockland Utilities 7/99. Commercial rev. ratio (55%) compares with 32% for the industry. Noncome taxes and avg. price per kilowatt-hour are among the highest in U.S. Fuel costs: 55% of revs.; labor costs, 14%. 2000 reported deprec. rate: 3.7%. Est'd plant age: 9 years. In '00, purch. almost all energy it sold on firm contracts with nonutility generators. Has 14,463 empls, 109,460 common shareholders. Chmn., CEO & Pres.: Eugene R. McGrath. Inc.: N.Y. Add.: 4 Irving Place, New York, N.Y. 10003. Tel.: 212-460-3903. Internet: www.coned.com.

Consolidated Edison and Northeast Utilities have filed lawsuits against each other over their failed merger. ED asked a federal district court to release it from all obligations it had to NU under their 1999 merger agreement and to protect it from any damages sought by NU. It claimed that NU's power marketing subsidiary was mismanaged and was at risk of not having enough power to serve NU's Connecticut Light & Power subsidiary at profitable prices starting in 2002. NU countersued ED for $1 billion in the same court, on the grounds that its shareholders would have received an acquisition premium of that amount if the merger had been consummated. It stated further that ED refused to commit to the original terms, but sought to lower the agreed-upon sales price. In order to avoid lengthy and costly court hearings, we think the parties might negotiate a settlement.
The company has a contract to sell its nuclear station. The sale includes the 1,000 megawatt Indian Point 2 plant and the retired unit 1 facility. Entergy has agreed to pay $502 million for both plants and $100 million for nuclear fuel. The sale will be for about book value. Entergy will sell the output of unit 2 to Con Edison at below-market prices through the end of 2004. That will cushion the company against unexpected energy price spikes. After the deal is consummated, ED will be primarily a regulated transmission and distribution company with a few small investments in noncore assets.
We look for steady, but slow, earnings gains to 2004-2006. Last year's charges related to the basically dead NU merger and disallowed replacement power costs for Indian Point 2 will be absent this year. But these positives will be reduced somewhat by lower electric rates and higher interest expense. All told, we estimate a 19% rise in 2001 earnings to $3.25 a share. The completion of two merchant plants next year points to an earnings uptick in 2002.
The year-ahead yield is a full percentage point above the industry norm. Moreover, dividend growth prospects to the 2004-2006 are near those of the group. That might be sufficient reason to attract conservative utility investors because of the company's gilt-edged finances.
Arthur H. Medalie   *September 7, 2001*

(A) EPS diluted. Next report due late Oct. (B) Next dividend meeting about Oct. 18. Goes ex about Nov. 12. Dividend payment dates: Mar. 15, June 15, Sept. 15, Dec. 15. ■ = Div'd reinvest. plan avail. (C) Includes intangibles. In '00: $7.58/sh. (D) Rate base: net original cost. Rate all'd elec. common equity: '97, 12.9%; earned on '00 average common equity: 10.7%. Regulatory Climate: Average. (E) In millions, adjusted for stock split.

Company's Financial Strength A++
Stock's Price Stability 95
Price Growth Persistence 25
Earnings Predictability 90

© 2001, Value Line Publishing, Inc. All rights reserved. Factual material is obtained from sources believed to be reliable and is provided without warranties of any kind. THE PUBLISHER IS NOT RESPONSIBLE FOR ANY ERRORS OR OMISSIONS HEREIN. This publication is strictly for subscriber's own, non-commercial, internal use. No part of it may be reproduced, resold, stored or transmitted in any printed, electronic or other form, or used for generating or marketing any printed or electronic publication, service or product.

To subscribe call 1-800-833-0046.

Figure 15

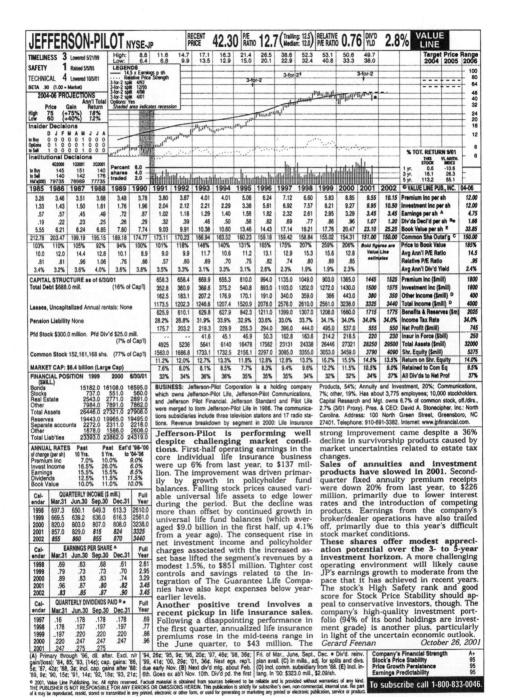

Figure 15

JEFFERSON-PILOT NYSE-JP

RECENT PRICE 42.30 | P/E RATIO 12.7 (Trailing: 12.5; Median: 12.0) | RELATIVE P/E RATIO 0.76 | DIV'D YLD 2.8% | VALUE LINE

TIMELINESS 3 Lowered 5/21/99
SAFETY 1 Raised 5/5/95
TECHNICAL 4 Lowered 10/5/01
BETA .90 (1.00 = Market)

	1990	1991	1992	1993	1994	1995	1996	1997	1998	1999	2000	2001
High:	8.8	11.6	14.7	17.1	16.3	21.4	26.5	38.6	52.3	53.1	50.6	49.7
Low:	6.4	6.8	9.9	13.5	12.9	15.0	20.1	22.9	32.4	40.8	33.3	38.0

2004-06 PROJECTIONS

	Price	Gain	Ann'l Total Return
High	75	(+75%)	*18%*
Low	60	(+40%)	*12%*

Insider Decisions

	D	J	F	M	A	M	J	J	A
to Buy	0	0	0	0	0	1	0	0	0
Options	0	1	0	0	0	1	0	0	0
to Sell	1	0	0	0	0	1	0	0	0

Institutional Decisions

	4Q2000	1Q2001	2Q2001
to Buy	145	151	140
to Sell	140	142	176
Hld's(000)	79735	76989	77735

1985	1986	1987	1988	1989	1990	1991	1992	1993	1994	1995	1996	1997	1998	1999	2000	2001	2002	© VALUE LINE PUB., INC.	04-06
3.26	3.46	3.51	3.68	3.48	3.78	3.80	3.87	4.01	4.01	5.06	6.24	7.12	6.60	5.83	8.85	*9.55*	*10.15*	Premium Inc per sh	*12.00*
1.33	1.43	1.50	1.61	1.76	1.96	2.04	2.12	2.21	2.29	3.38	5.61	6.92	7.57	8.21	9.27	*9.95*	*10.50*	Investment Inc per sh	*12.00*
.57	.57	.45	.49	.72	.87	1.02	1.18	1.29	1.40	1.58	1.82	2.32	2.61	2.95	3.29	*3.45*	*3.45*	Earnings per sh A	*4.75*
.19	.22	.23	.25	.26	.29	.32	.39	.46	.50	.56	.62	.69	.77	.86	.96	*1.07*	*1.20*	Div'ds Decl'd per sh B■	*1.66*
5.55	6.21	6.24	6.85	7.80	7.74	9.03	9.91	10.38	10.60	13.46	14.43	17.14	19.21	17.76	20.47	*23.10*	*25.25*	Book Value per sh E	*33.85*
212.78	203.47	199.19	195.15	189.18	174.77	173.11	170.23	166.94	163.52	160.23	159.18	159.42	158.84	155.02	154.31	*151.00*	*150.00*	Common Shs Outst'g C	*150.00*
103%	110%	105%	92%	94%	100%	101%	118%	146%	140%	131%	165%	175%	207%	259%	206%	*Bold figures are*	*Value Line*	Price to Book Value	*185%*
10.0	12.0	14.4	12.8	10.1	8.9	9.0	9.9	11.7	10.6	11.2	13.1	12.9	15.3	15.6	12.8	*estimates*		Avg Ann'l P/E Ratio	*14.5*
.81	.81	.96	1.06	.76	.66	.57	.60	.69	.70	.75	.82	.74	.80	.89	.85			Relative P/E Ratio	*.95*
3.4%	3.2%	3.6%	4.0%	3.6%	3.8%	3.5%	3.3%	3.1%	3.3%	3.1%	2.6%	2.3%	1.9%	1.9%	2.3%			Avg Ann'l Div'd Yield	*2.4%*

CAPITAL STRUCTURE as of 6/30/01
Total Debt $688.0 mill. (16% of Cap'l)

Leases, Uncapitalized Annual rentals: None

Pension Liability None

Pfd Stock $300.0 million. Pfd Div'd $25.0 mill. (7% of Cap'l)

Common Stock 152,161,168 shs. (77% of Cap'l)

MARKET CAP: $6.4 billion (Large Cap)

1991	1992	1993	1994	1995	1996	1997	1998	1999	2000	2001	2002	© VALUE LINE PUB., INC.	04-06
658.3	658.4	669.9	655.3	810.0	994.0	1135.0	1049.0	903.0	1365.0	*1445*	*1525*	Premium Inc ($mill)	*1800*
352.8	360.9	369.6	375.2	540.8	893.0	1103.0	1202.0	1272.0	1430.0	*1500*	*1575*	Investment Inc ($mill)	*1800*
162.5	183.1	207.2	176.9	170.1	191.0	340.0	359.0	386	443.0	*380*	*350*	Other Income ($mill) D	*400*
1173.5	1202.3	1246.6	1207.4	1520.9	2078.0	2578.0	2610.0	2561.0	3238.0	*3325*	*3440*	Total Income ($mill) D	*4000*
625.9	610.1	629.8	627.9	842.3	1211.0	1399.0	1307.0	1208.0	1660.0	*1715*	*1775*	Benefits & Reserves ($m)	*2025*
28.2%	28.8%	31.9%	33.9%	32.9%	33.6%	33.0%	33.7%	34.1%	34.0%	*34.0%*	*34.0%*	Income Tax Rate	*34.0%*
175.7	203.2	219.3	229.9	255.3	294.0	396.0	444.0	495.0	537.0	*555*	*550*	Net Profit ($mill)	*745*
--	--	41.6	45.1	46.9	50.3	162.8	163.6	214.2	218.5	*220*	*230*	Insur in Force ($bill)	*250*
4925	5236	5641	6140	16478	17562	23131	24338	26446	27321	*28250*	*29500*	Total Assets ($mill)	*32000*
1563.0	1686.8	1733.1	1732.5	2156.1	2297.0	3085.0	3355.0	3053.0	3459.0	*3790*	*4090*	Shr. Equity ($mill)	*5375*
11.2%	12.0%	12.7%	13.3%	11.8%	12.8%	12.8%	13.2%	16.2%	15.5%	*14.5%*	*13.5%*	Return on Shr. Equity	*14.0%*
7.6%	8.0%	8.1%	8.5%	7.7%	8.3%	9.4%	9.6%	12.2%	11.5%	*10.5%*	*9.0%*	Retained to Com Eq	*9.5%*
33%	34%	36%	36%	35%	35%	35%	34%	32%	32%	*34%*	*37%*	All Div'ds to Net Prof	*37%*

FINANCIAL POSITION ($MILL.)	1999	2000	6/30/01
Bonds	15182.0	16108.0	16595.0
Stocks	737.0	551.0	560.0
Real Estate	2543.0	2771.0	2891.0
Other	7984.0	7891.0	7862.0
Total Assets	26446.0	27321.0	27908.0
Reserves	19443.0	19965.0	19495.0
Separate accounts	2272.0	2311.0	2218.0
Other	1678.0	1586.0	2606.0
Total Liab'ties	23393.0	23862.0	24319.0

ANNUAL RATES of change (per sh)	Past 10 Yrs.	Past 5 Yrs.	Est'd '98-'00 to '04-'06
Premium Inc	7.0%	10.0%	*9.0%*
Invest Income	16.5%	26.0%	*6.0%*
Earnings	15.5%	15.5%	*8.5%*
Dividends	12.5%	11.5%	*11.5%*
Book Value	10.0%	11.0%	*10.0%*

Calendar	QUARTERLY INCOME ($ mill.) Mar.31	Jun.30	Sep.30	Dec.31	Full Year
1998	697.3	650.1	649.3	613.3	2610.0
1999	669.5	639.2	636.0	616.3	2561.0
2000	820.0	803.0	807.0	808.0	3238.0
2001	857.0	829.0	*815*	*824*	*3325*
2002	*855*	*860*	*855*	*870*	*3440*

Calendar	EARNINGS PER SHARE A Mar.31	Jun.30	Sep.30	Dec.31	Full Year
1998	.69	.63	.68	.61	2.61
1999	.79	.73	.73	.70	2.95
2000	.89	.83	.83	.74	3.29
2001	.96	.87	*.80*	*.82*	*3.45*
2002	*.83*	*.85*	*.87*	*.90*	*3.45*

Calendar	QUARTERLY DIVIDENDS PAID B ■ Mar.31	Jun.30	Sep.30	Dec.31	Full Year
1997	.16	.178	.178	.178	.69
1998	.178	.197	.197	.197	.77
1999	..197	.220	.220	.220	.86
2000	.220	.247	.247	.247	.96
2001	.247	.275	.275		

BUSINESS: Jefferson-Pilot Corporation is a holding company which owns Jefferson-Pilot Life, Jefferson-Pilot Communications, and Jefferson Pilot Financial. Jefferson Standard and Pilot Life were merged to form Jefferson-Pilot Life in 1986. The communications subsidiaries include three television stations and 17 radio stations. Revenue breakdown by segment in 2000: Life Insurance Products, 54%; Annuity and Investment, 20%; Communications, 7%; other, 19%. Has about 3,775 employees; 10,000 stockholders. Capital Research and Mgt. owns 6.7% of common stock, off./dirs., 2.7% (3/01 Proxy). Pres. & CEO: David A. Stonecipher. Inc.: North Carolina. Address: 100 North Green Street, Greensboro, NC 27401. Telephone: 910-691-3382. Internet: www.jpfinancial.com.

Jefferson-Pilot is performing well despite challenging market conditions. First-half operating earnings in the core individual life insurance business were up 6% from last year, to $137 million. The improvement was driven primarily by growth in policyholder fund balances. Falling stock prices caused variable universal life assets to edge lower during the period. But the decline was more than offset by continued growth in universal life fund balances (which averaged $9.0 billion in the first half, up 4.1% from a year ago). The consequent rise in net investment income and policyholder charges associated with the increased asset base lifted the segment's revenues by a modest 1.5%, to $851 million. Tighter cost controls and savings related to the integration of The Guarantee Life Companies have also kept expenses below year-earlier levels.

Another positive trend involves a recent pickup in life insurance sales. Following a disappointing performance in the first quarter, annualized life insurance premiums rose in the mid-teens range in the June quarter, to $43 million. The strong improvement came despite a 36% decline in survivorship products caused by market uncertainties related to estate tax changes.

Sales of annuities and investment products have slowed in 2001. Second-quarter fixed annuity premium receipts were down 20% from last year, to $226 million, primarily due to lower interest rates and the introduction of competing products. Earnings from the company's broker/dealer operations have also trailed off, primarily due to this year's difficult stock market conditions.

These shares offer modest appreciation potential over the 3- to 5-year investment horizon. A more challenging operating environment will likely cause JP's earnings growth to moderate from the pace that it has achieved in recent years. The stock's High Safety rank and good score for Stock Price Stability should appeal to conservative investors, though. The company's high-quality investment portfolio (94% of its bond holdings are investment grade) is another plus, particularly in light of the uncertain economic outlook.

Gerard Feenan *October 26, 2001*

(A) Primary through '96, dil. after. Excl. n/r gain/(loss): '84, 85; '93, (14¢); cap. gains: '86, 5¢; '87, 42¢; '88, 3¢; incl. cap. gains after '88: '89, 9¢; '90, 15¢; '91, 14¢; '92, 18¢; '93, 21¢; '94, 26¢; '95, 9¢; '96, 20¢; '97, 46¢; '98, 36¢; '99, 41¢; '00, 29¢; '01, 36¢. Next egs. rep't. due early Nov. (B) Next div'd mtg. about Feb. 6th. Goes ex ab't Nov. 10th. Div'd pd. the first Fri. of Mar., June, Sept., Dec. ■ Div'd. reinv. plan avail. (C) In mills., adj. for splits and divs. (D) Incl. comm. subsidiary from '88. (E) Incl. intang. In '00: $323.0 mill., $2.09/sh.

Company's Financial Strength	A+
Stock's Price Stability	95
Price Growth Persistence	95
Earnings Predictability	95

Things Are not Always What They Seem

We are all aware that a big name does not always mean prosperity. The problems of IBM, GM, Sears, Westinghouse, and Eastman Kodak, among others, have been the subject of news stories for several years. Even without this publicity a careful investor like I who values consistency and reviewed their price performance, sales, earnings, and dividend growth, would have avoided these companies. That is not to say that some or all of them may not do well in the future. It is just that their future is uncertain and the prudent investor wants something closer to a sure thing. But this is only half the picture. There are also companies whose names and types of business may not seem especially attractive that are very solid and profitable companies. Look up Tootsie Roll, Wrigley, and Automatic Data Processing. These companies, and many more like them, do not worry about glamour. They just make money. Of course there is no guarantee that one or more will not suffer a reverse, but the odds are in their favor.

Do not Fall in Love

With a stock, that is. This is a very common problem. A stock has done well for years, but your question should be, "What has it done for me lately?" At least 1,000 times a day a husband, in contemplation of death, says to his wife, "Mary, whatever you do, never sell the IBM (or the GM, or the Sears, or whatever). It has always been good to us and it is as solid as Gibraltar. If it goes bad, the whole country will go." This attitude is not confined to innocent and inexperienced investors. On the day IBM collapsed, in the fall of 1992, several analysts in New York were recommending it as a buy and only one advised selling it. IBM's deterioration had been a matter of public record in financial news for ten years. I do not like to be uncharitable, but the failure of investors, especially the professionals, to recognize and face the facts is inexcusable. If you mishandle your investments, the Lord will forgive you, but the market won't. Your soul will be in great shape, but you may be a little short of cash.

* * *

A WILD RIDE

In connection with stock selection I had an experience many years ago that was not only interesting but also instructive. It was in September 1959, I believe. For some foolish reason I had sold out my stocks and was all in cash. I happened to notice a quarterly earnings report of Wickes and it looked exceptionally good at $10, about 4 or 5 times earnings, as I recall. I then lived in Saginaw, Michigan and Wickes was a very old, very respected local manufacturer. I had never thought of it as an investment, although my uncle had been a director of the company for many years. I talked to my broker and decided to invest some of my loose cash in Wickes, by then at $11. With good earnings and a low P/E I expected a good dividend and that it might double in price in 5 years or so, good for the long term.

But it kept going up and I bought more at $12 and then $14. It still seemed a bargain. It kept going up and I kept buying more until I ran out of cash at $22. You must understand I was young and foolish and I do not now recommend any such transaction. But it still kept going up, and every couple of days I would drop in to chat with my broker. By this time all the tape watchers in the office knew what was going on and covertly watched me when I came in. I don't know whether they expected me to launch another financial coup or were just waiting for the bubble to burst.

By the time it got to 30 I knew it was no bargain. I would have been prudent to sell but for one thing. In those days there was no tax on long term capital gains, then defined as over six months, so it was not merely a matter of price, but time was important, too. I was in no danger of actually losing money and, with two months more to go I was determined to avoid the tax. My innocent investment had turned into a high stakes (for me) gamble.

At the end of January, with Wickes at $32, my broker called, "Frank (the manager) wants to talk to you." I walked the block from my office and the audience was intrigued to see me go to the manager's office. Frank said, "I think you should sell your Wickes." "What? Sell it short term? No way." "Well", said Frank, "you know their earnings report is coming out next week." "Anything wrong with the earnings?" "Oh no, but sometimes investors expect more and that hurts the price." I was adamant. I was not going to pay any capital gains tax. But they had figured out a way to avoid it. It was a commodity hedge. I was to buy so many contracts of soybeans and sell the same number. They explained the complex transaction. I could not make heads or tails of the explanation and refused to sell.

The next couple of months were a nervous time for me. Not that I could have lost, but you can get pretty attached to a paper profit. It would feel like a loss. But Wickes still kept going up 35 - 38 - 40. There were still investors around who were crazier than I was. Finally the six months was up with Wickes at 45. I sold it out at the speed of light. For the next few days it still went up until it got to 48. It then hit the skids and never recovered.

This shows how an innocent bystander can become embroiled in wild speculation. I was not seeking fame, adventure or sudden wealth. When I first bought the stock I had no idea it would skyrocket. It seemed like a good solid stock that I could hold for the long pull, but as it kept going up, I developed a fever. It cured me however. I didn't want to go through that again, but I did enjoy our month long motor trip through Europe in our new Mercedes.

CHAPTER 11

MORE ABOUT P/E
(Price/Earnings)

Missed Opportunity?

Seven years ago, after my brother's death, my sister in law asked me to review her investment portfolio. I noticed that it contained quite a large investment in Microsoft, which had done very well but paid no dividend and had not fully demonstrated its long term staying power. I commented that I would not buy the stock though it had done so well. I would not sell it either, since I have an ironclad rule that I never sell a winner. Since then its value has increased 27 fold. Did I make a mistake in not buying it? Things look very different with hindsight. Under similar circumstances I would do the same today.

The Mistake

I do not want to undermine my conservative principles and encourage you to speculate. My judgment was correct. While I missed a good thing, if I had made other similar investments, I would surely have lost heavily. This was not a momentary window of opportunity. The window has been open for seven years, and I believe it is still open. Had I followed Microsoft carefully, I would have recognized when it matured and became a solid high quality investment grade security. Had I bought it 4 or 5 years ago, I would have had most of the profit without the risk. My mistake was in missing the later opportunities.

A Slow Learner

For the past 7 years I have ignored Microsoft, partly because of an aversion to high tech, partly from a lack of understanding its business, and mostly because the P/E was so high I thought it was overpriced. I use MSFT as an example, but there were a number of other stocks I excluded for similar reasons. Over the past year or so it began to penetrate my thick skull that some high tech companies and some with very high P/Es are very profitable investments and apparently not particularly risky.

A Gradual Awakening

My attitude toward a high P/E obviously needed revision. I had never been comfortable in trying to establish any kind of numerical guidelines, but for an inexperienced investor this is an area for caution. But, for the more experienced investor, and for my own use as well, I decided to use my very limited mathematical resources to clarify the matter. It is certain that this problem has been noticed, and solved, by many sophisticated investors. Since I am unaware of their solutions, I can only offer my own.

Proceed with Caution

This is for those who want to pursue further the question, how high a P/E can be justified? I find this a very difficult subject to tackle, but the experienced investor can find study of the subject quite rewarding if he approaches it with caution.

Earnings are the Key

We all understand, or we should, earnings are the principal factor that determines a company's value and therefore the price of its stock. A company that has no ability to earn a profit is only worth what its real estate, machinery, etc. can be sold for in liquidation. If a company is making a profit, its current earnings are interesting, but its price depends more on the investor perception of its future profit, its earnings growth rate, especially for future periods of 5, 10, or 20 years.

Earnings Growth and the PE

A mathematician and scholar, I am neither, could figure out what P/E an investor would pay for a company with no earnings growth. It should then be possible to figure the break even P/E for a company with 5% growth for a 5 year period or one with 12% growth for 10 years. I do not like this approach because there are too many uncertainties and because a numerical formula gives a false impression of precision.

Do we give up?

We do not. But the only alternative is to make some kind of use of these objectionable uncertainties, the imprecise predictions and extrapolations. At first glance this may seem hopeless, but how often do we encounter a sure thing? Our whole environment is one uncertainty after another, but we are able to deal with them because we know they are uncertain. We do not know what an adjacent driver will do so we give him a wide berth and keep an eye on him. Once we understand the characteristics of the tools we have to work with we can plan how to use them.

Measuring Uncertainty

This seems a contradiction, how can we measure something amorphous? Well, perhaps evaluate is a better word. When considering the future success of a business, there are many possible indicators that we can weigh. How long has it been in business? How profitable is it? How consistent is it? Are future prospects good? When all our questions are answered we have formed a pretty good picture of the company and are prepared to form our own odds on the company's future.

The Approach

Possibly due to limits on my mental capacity, I can not devise an elegant formula or method to measure the appropriate P/E for a company, so I shall have to use "Brute Force". The approach that I will use is to compare two companies. For example, you might want to decide which of two companies to buy. Or you might select one company as a standard and compare any candidates for purchase to that one as a standard.

The Mechanics of Comparison - Example #1

Let us first try two stocks about as different as you can get. There is one similarity, both have the top rating of A++ for financial strength. I shall compare Consolidated Edison with Microsoft.

TABLE 18
At the Start

STOCK	10 YEAR EARNINGS GROWTH	PRICE	# SHARES	VALUE	DIV	INCOME
CON ED	3.0%	26	19,231	500,086	2.08	40,000
MSFT	48%	72½	6,896	499,960	0	0

AFTER 5 YEARS

STOCK	ESTIMATED CURRENT EARNINGS GROWTH	PRICE	# SHARES	VALUE	DIV	INCOME
CON ED	3.0%	30	19,231	576,930	2.41	46,347
MSFT	30%	269	6,896	1,855,024	0	0

AFTER 10 YEARS

STOCK	ESTIMATED CURRENT EARNINGS GROWTH	PRICE	# SHARES	VALUE	DIV	INCOME
CON ED	3.0%	35	19,231	673,085	2.79	53,654
MSFT	20%	669	6,896	4,613,424	0	0

In making this comparison and projecting future growth I noted that the electric utility industry has had a 3% growth rate for many years, so I left it at 3 for the projections. As to Microsoft, it obviously can not maintain a 48% rate. The question is how far it will drop and how soon. It is a very powerful company and strongly entrenched in the PC industry and I believe its decline will be slow and orderly. Trying to be conservative, I have estimated its growth at 30% for the next 5 years and 20% for the following 5. That is about as long as I would make even a tentative estimate in that industry. For both companies I have estimated stock prices and dividends will grow at the same pace as earnings.

Results #1

For a worker saving for retirement there is only one choice. No one of sound mind could hesitate. Even if Con Ed did twice as well, which I can hardly imagine, it would be hard to construct any reasonable scenario that would not show Microsoft many times better. But what happens when a retiree needs income? I can picture an old codger, perhaps nearly as old as I am, grumbling, "I'm sticking with Con Ed. At least they pay a good dividend, I can not eat paper profits." Unfortunately this old gentleman has forgotten how to add and subtract. For the first 5 years he could have sold enough to equal his dividend plus capital gains tax and for the next 5 years he could have taken 100,000 a year or twice that. Well this is not a typical comparison an investor would make, but it's a good demonstration.

Example #2

In this case suppose I am a serious investor and I look for excellent performance, but I do not want to pay too much for it. I like General Electric and I have selected it as a standard. I like Coca Cola, but its P/E, at 39, seems very high. Should I buy it?

TABLE 19
At the Start

STOCK	10 YEAR EARNINGS GROWTH	PRICE	# SHARES	VALUE	DIV	INCOME
GE	11%	104	4,808	500,032	1.88	9,039
KO	18%	52	9,615	499,980	.50	4,808

AFTER 5 YEARS

STOCK	ESTIMATED CURRENT EARNINGS GROWTH	PRICE	# SHARES	VALUE	DIV	INCOME
GE	11%	175	4,808	841,400	3.17	15,241
KO	18%	119	9,615	1,144,185	1.14	10,961

AFTER 10 YEARS

STOCK	ESTIMATED CURRENT EARNINGS GROWTH	PRICE	# SHARES	VALUE	DIV	INCOME
GE	11%	295	4,808	1,418,360	5.34	29,675
KO	18%	272	9,615	2,615,280	2.60	24,999

Result #2

This is more interesting. I saw no reason to change the earnings growth rates of either stock. For a person saving for retirement, while both stocks are much better than average, the odds favor Coke even with a P/E spread of 39 to 24. If people are already retired and need income, especially if their life expectancy is less than 15 years, they might choose GE, but they would be well off either way.

Even After Seven Years

Four months ago I was talking to a friend about Microsoft's spectacular performance over the past 10 years and he asked, ironically, "What is the next Microsoft?" I could not answer that but I said the old Microsoft was still doing very well. This discussion decided me to buy it even though it was at its all time high. In the subsequent 4 months it has gone up 46%. It surely will not maintain such a pace and there will inevitably be downs as well as ups. Every investor should know that, while there is a limit to how much you can lose, there is no such limit on gains.

The Chain saw

This device is like a chain saw. It is not for the casual user, and even an experienced investor should use it with care. I considered omitting this chapter completely, because I know there are optimists who will get burned, but I have to tell it like it is, as best I can. There must be very many savvy investors using a similar device.

CHAPTER 12

Electric Utilities

Sales Pressure

I should not have to write this chapter. You already know better than to invest in these shares. But it is a fact of life that there are people who are paid large sums of money for their ability to persuade you to buy things with which you would be better off. This is one of the high profile investments widely recommended and peddled by various types of salesmen, and this chapter is sort of a vaccine, intended to reinforce your immunity. Repetition can be helpful. I remember the instructional method used in Navy training classes during WWII. The instructor told you what he was going to tell you, then he told you, and finally he told you what he had told you. The method is still alive and well in this book.

Why Single Out the Electrics?

There are many companies and other industries that are unsuitable for our purposes. But these shares are very attractive to unsophisticated investors, especially retirees. They have trouble distinguishing yield from earnings.

Murder by Slow Strangulation

These stocks have one outstanding feature that makes them attractive to some investors - a relatively high yield. What is wrong with that? It sounds pretty good. There are two ways to increase yield, raise the dividend or lower the stock price. The low price of these stocks is no bargain. Instead it demonstrates that many investors avoid such slow growth as they offer. Salespeople find that the low price and high yield are strong selling points, and few salespeople would mention inflation or slow growth. It is difficult to cure this disease because the incubation period is so long. The slow strangulation takes a few years to clamp down and by then the victim can not recognize the cause.

Let's Look at the Record

Al Smith had it right, let us forget the chin music and look at the record. Following is a list of 44 electric utilities. To list them all would be overkill, so this list is all of them listed in Value Line from the central area of the country. Bearing in mind the tentative standards you have already adopted, look over this list and see how many of them you want to invest in.

TABLE 20
Percent Annual Increase Last 10 Years

COMPANY	YIELD	EARNING	DIVIDENDS	REVENUES	BOOK VALUE
CIPSCO	6.0%	2.0	2.5	1.5	2.5
CMS ENERGY	3.0	-4.5	-15.0	-1.0	-7.0
CENTERIOR EN'GY	6.2	-12.6	-3.6	-.9	?
CENTRAL & S.W.	5.4	4.5	6.5	3.0	5.5
CENTRAL LA. EL	6.0	3.0	6.0	1.5	6.0
CILCORP	6.6	.5	3.0	2.0	2.5
CINCINNATI G&E	6.1	3.5	1.5	-1.5	3.5
COMMONW. ED.	5.7	-3.0	-6.1	-.5	.5
DPL	5.8	2.5	3.0	-1.5	2.5
DETROIT ED.	7.3	7.0	1.5	1.5	1.0
EL PASO EL.	-0-	-	-	-	-
EMPIRE DIST	6.7	4.5	5.5	.5	5.0
ENTERGY CORP.	5.0	1.0	-2.5	.5	3.0
GULF ST UTIL	-0	-3.0	-	-2.5	1.5
HOUSTON IND	6.5	1.5	4.0	12.0	1.5
IES IND	6.8	-1.0	2.0	2.5	1.0
ILLINOIS POWER	3.9	-11.5	-16.5	-2.5	-1.5
INTERSTATE POW	6.5	1.5	2.5	-.5	1.5
IOWA-ILLINOIS	7.2	.5	4.5	-.5	4.0
IPALCO ENTERPR	6.1	4.5	4.5	3.0	5.0
KUENERGY CORP	5.7	6.5	3.5	.5	3.5
KANSAS CITY PWR	6.5	.5	4.0	1.5	2.5
LG&E ELECTRIC	5.3	3.5	3.0	-	3.0
MDU RESOURCES	4.9	2.0	4.0	1.0	3.5
MIDWEST RES.	6.4	-2.4	-.9	1.4	.6
MINNESOTA POWER	6.3	3.5	6.0	.5	3.5
NIPSCO IND	4.6	4.5	-2.5	-3.0	-.5
NORTHERN STATES'	6.1	3.5	6.5	4.5	5.5
NORTWESTERN P.S.	5.8	5.0	5.0	1.0	3.5
OHIO EDISON	6.5	-1.8	-1.8	-1.0	.5
OKLAHOMA G&E	7.2	3.5	4.5	3.0	3.0
OTTERTAIL POWER	5.4	6.0	3.5	2.5	2.0
PSI RESOURCES	4.7	-6.0	-10.0	1.0	-7.5
ST. JOE L&P	6.4	5.5	6.5	2.0	5.5
SO. IND. G&E	5.0	6.0	8.0	2.5	5.5
S.W. PUB. SERV.	7.1	1.4	4.0	.5	4.0
TNP ENTERPRISES	5.9	1.5	5.0	-2.0	5.0
TEXAS UTILITIES	7.0	-	4.5	-1.0	3.0
UNION ELECTRIC	6.2	3.0	3.5	3.0	2.5
UTILCORP	5.3	6.0	13.0	8.5	9.0
WPL HOLDINGS	5.9	5.0	6.0	3.0	5.0
WESRTERN RES.	5.7	3.0	5.5	8.0	5.0
WISC ENERGY'	5.1	6.0	7.5	2.0	7.0
WISCONSIN P.S.	5.5	3.5	6.5	3.0	4.5

How Much Good News?

The first column of figures, the yields, looks attractive and, for most of the companies, that is the last of the good news. But this is about as far as most utility investors look. Eat, drink, and be merry, for tomorrow we die. Maybe, however, they will live, and, even though they do not know the bad news yet, they will have to live with it, probably for many years. The second column is more sobering. The 10 year average earnings growth ranges from 7% to a minus 12.6%, averaging around 3%, less than my own minimum standard and, worse yet, it is a little below the average inflation rate. It is not exactly a hemorrhage, they are just bleeding to death more slowly. To a long-term investor, this is a sad group. While it is not necessary to look past earnings, you will note many other problems in these companies.

The Cause of the Problem

Why is this group so unproductive? Everybody has to have electricity. It is usually a monopoly and people pay their bills every month. This should be a profitable business. Aside from the usual percentage of poor managers, there are external factors that are almost insuperable. Public utility commissions that are sensative to public opinion control their rates. Except for the shareholders, <u>nobody</u> wants higher rates. There are millions of people, however, who think the utilities are rich and are making excessive profits. They are well organized and continually press the regulators to <u>reduce</u> rates. As a result many utility regulators keep rates as low as possible without actually putting the companies out of business. These poor results are also the fault of investors. The regulators know from experience that there are many investors who will tolerate low <u>total</u> returns from utilities as long as dividends are adequate. If investors refused to support marginal companies, regulators would be forced to allow better returns.

The Nuclear Problem

Another serious problem is nuclear power. While people are generally more apprehensive about the possibility of a nuclear accident, a local Chernobyl, there may be a more serious problem for the stockholders, and it is no accident. Nuclear power plants, like conventional ones, eventually wear out, becoming inefficient and obsolete. These plants are expensive to build and to replace, but the real cost is in deactivating them and making the abandoned site secure and safe. Without going into the gruesome details, it appears that closing it down will cost much more than building it in the first place, and I question whether any utility is, or will be, in a position to bear that expense.

A Common Problem

The problem of inadequate earnings is common to all these companies, but those that operate nuclear plants bear a much greater burden.

CHAPTER 13

The Mechanics of Investing

Many readers will be thoroughly familiar with this subject, but for some, the details of investing may seem quite mysterious.

Where to Start

Nearly all buying and selling of stock is handled by stockbrokers. There are exceptions under special circumstances, which I will explain later, but you will probably prefer to use a broker. Brokers are licensed professionals, generally employees of large brokerage firms. They are trained to execute security transactions and have ready access to the stock markets. They can quickly match potential buyers and sellers at a market price fair to both.

Two Kinds of Brokers

A broker's basic function is to facilitate and expedite buying and selling of securities. This function is somewhat comparable to completing a telephone connection and, in the same way it has been mechanized with a dramatic reduction in cost of executing the transactions. The price of the service to the customer does not always reflect this reduction. While cost increases are passed along immediately, businesses are often reluctant to lower prices unless forced to by stiff competition. They would rather increase services, and that has been the rule in the brokerage industry. Predictably the wide profit margin has created an opportunity for entrepreneurs who provide the basic service at a <u>much</u> lower price. They are called "discount brokers". Although the adjective "discount" often implies a service that is substandard, my own experience with them has been perfectly satisfactory. There are many investors who want additional service from a broker. They want advice and information, personal attention, and a more luxurious ambiance. Ambiance costs money making the fees of a "full service" broker from perhaps three to ten times those of the discount broker.

Which to Choose?

Each type of broker has advantages and disadvantages. Starting off, you will have to make a decision. It is not irrevocable and it is much easier to change brokers than you would expect. You just sign an authorization form and your new broker will transfer your securities to your new account.

The Discount Broker

Advantages:

1. Cost. Transaction fees vary from about 1/2% to 1% of the amount of the trade, compared to 2% to 3% for the full service broker. <u>CAUTION</u>: Both kinds of brokers have minimum commissions and, if you intend to make a trade valued at less than $2,000 or $3,000, ask in advance what the commission will be.

2. Orders are executed quickly and accurately and their completion is reported promptly by telephone.

3. A number of services beside execution of orders are offered. Typically, a discount broker will hold your securities in your federally insured account, send you monthly statements showing the status of your account, provide a money market fund which can be used to accumulate dividends or deposits, and quote current market prices of stocks. These services are usually without any additional charge.

4. Virtually the same services as the full service variety are offered. This may include investment advice, although I am not at all sure that investment advice from a broker is an advantage. Not surprisingly, their fees are higher than straight discount brokers and lower than full service. I would call these <u>semi</u>-discount brokers. Although none are as large as the biggest brokers, some are becoming stiff competitors and are gaining market share. It is only a question of time before the semi-discounters, and close on their heels, the discount brokers, will force a substantial reduction in the fees charged by all brokers.

Disadvantage:

1. Impersonal atmosphere. Generally you call an 800 number and talk to someone you do not know. You feel as if you are merely an account number. There is little chit-chat, it is all business and no advice. You are treated like a businessperson. You know what you are doing and are no more interested in wasting time than they are. Many investors who are inexperienced or who lack confidence want the reassurance of contact with a person they know, and they may also want advice.

The big advantage is the very low cost. The disadvantage is the impersonal business atmosphere compared to a friendly personal relationship.

The Full Service Broker

Advantages:

1. The investor can go into the office, sit down at the broker's desk, and talk face to face. You feel as if you are traveling first class.

2. Like the discount broker, trades are well handled.

3. These companies have research departments at the home office and are able to give their customers detailed, up to date information on most companies whose shares are publicly traded.

4. The broker will also, if asked, and very likely even if not asked, advise customers what to buy or sell. Again this is a questionable advantage.

Disadvantages:

1. The very high commission charges. The amount of the charge is the same whether you want advice or investment information or not. This is unattractive to anyone who makes his or her own decisions.

2. Another problem is the qualifications of the broker giving the advice. Much of the advice given by a broker is from a flyer from headquarters. If a million investors get the same advice on the same day, their concerted response might change the situation.

3. There is an inevitable conflict of interest whenever an adviser is also a salesman, and this conflict is exacerbated when it is a commission salesman. This conflict is even worse than it looks. Because commissions on different securities are different, some sales are much more profitable for the salesman. Most customers don't know anything about this.

4. Aside from the broker, the broker's employer also has a financial interest in these transaction, often not evident and quite different from the customer or even the broker.

5. In recent years full service brokers have begun to add additional special charges like surcharges if you wish a stock certificate or if your trading does not generate enough revenue in commissions.

All things considered, it is my view that those who can handle their own affairs will be better off with a discount broker. A full service broker is a kind of nurse. If you are physically disabled, you need a nurse. If you are mentally or emotionally disabled, you may need a full service broker. There is another group that might warrant this service. Those are people whose work is so demanding that they don't have the time or energy to devote to their investments.

Selecting a Broker

Perhaps a friend can recommend a suitable broker. If not, they can be found in the telephone Yellow Pages under Stockbrokers or in advertisements in financial newspapers or the business section of most metropolitan newspapers. Make sure the broker is a member of the National Association of Security Dealers (NASD) and is covered by SIPC, the Federal Government insurance. Discount brokers often advertise in the newspaper, but there are hundreds of them and their commissions and services vary widely. If you don't know someone who can recommend one, or even if you do, it would be a good idea to consult "The Discount Brokerage Directory and Survey" by Mark Coler. It will give you a pretty good idea of what kind of service you will get and what it will cost. This book will probably be available at your public library,

After you Select

When you have decided on a broker, call and ask for an application. The broker will want credit information, probably a bank reference. If you decide on a broker you do not know, you can also ask for   the broker's bank reference, and check it. If you have an account with another broker and wish the stocks held in that account transferred to your new broker, the new broker will make the necessary arrangements.

Making a trade

When your account is opened and you want to buy or sell stock, call the broker, give your account number, and place your order. The broker will call back promptly and tell you your order has been executed and the price. If it is a sale, and you hold the certificate, you must provide the stock certificate, properly endorsed, within 3 business days of the trade date, and the broker will pay you the proceeds in the same interval. If it is a purchase, the broker will notify you promptly in writing of the total cost, and it is your responsibility to pay for it within the same 3 business days after the trade.

Different Types of Orders

There are different ways to place an order. A "market" order will be executed immediately at the current market price. Some investors try to get a little advantage by specifying the price a little below market on a buy order or a little above on a sale. This often works and may save you an eighth or a quarter per share. However, if the price goes the wrong way, there will be no execution and you will be left with a pending order that you will eventually have to cancel and give a new order at a less favorable price. There is nothing wrong with this tactic, but your potential gain is small while the potential loss, although probably small, can be substantial.

Street Name or Certificate?

Usually brokers will hold your stock in their own name (street name) and will show it on your monthly statement. It is very safe being insured not only by the SIPC, federal insurance, but many brokers provide supplemental insurance. Make sure that your account is adequately insured. It is usually best to have the broker keep your stock and eliminate the nuisance of mailing certificates when you sell. There are two circumstances that might influence you to keep certificates. First, if you want automatic reinvestment of dividends, the stock must be registered in your name. Many brokers, including discount, furnish a similar service, but the cost is much higher, especially if the amount reinvested is small. The second is for use as collateral for a bank loan. This will usually result in a lower interest rate and avoids some of the expense and red tape associated with loans on real estate. If you decide to hold your own certificates, remember they are very important documents and should be kept in your safe deposit box.

CHAPTER 14

Building a Portfolio

How you build your portfolio depends on from where you are starting.

If you are already an Investor

Review each of your present holdings to see how they measure up to the standards you have established and to determine whether they are well diversified as to companies and industries. It is also desirable to keep the number of companies represented to a manageable size. Ten to fifteen stocks are easier to manage than 20 or 30. There is less paperwork and fewer companies to keep track of. You will probably want to avoid very small holdings. They take as much time to manage as your principal investments and consume your time and energy out of all proportion to there value to you.

Don't be Discouraged

It is quite possible that some of your holdings will not measure up to your criteria. You may even have some bonds, heaven forbid! You may perhaps have mutual funds. You already know why I do not like bonds, and I shall have something to say about mutual funds later. For now all I shall say is that mutual funds under perform the market averages and undermine one of my basic principles that all investors should make their own investment decisions, and not have to pay management fees every year for a service they should not need. Whatever the irregularities, they are just problems to work on, not to worry about. It does require action, but first careful planning. Do not abandon ship until you strap on your life jacket. Take a fresh piece of paper and put down an ideal portfolio consistent with the present value of your holdings, what you would like to work toward. Some of your present issues will probably be on the list. You then need to plan a deliberate and orderly way to get from here to there. If some of the issues you want to replace are bonds or stocks that have little or no capital gains you can move as soon as you decide on the replacements. However, there may be some stocks you wish to replace that have substantial gains. For tax reasons you may wish to sell these piecemeal. This will be a challenging project and may keep you out of mischief for several years. While we are thinking about the problem of capital gains, do not forget that capital losses, rare I hope, can be used to offset capital gains. If you have no gains or if the loss exceeds the gain, losses can to a limited extent offset other income. Remember when reinvesting the proceeds from a gain to put aside enough to cover the capital gains tax.

Diversification

This should be an integral part of your restructuring, even though it may be hard to accept the importance of selling a very good stock. This move is not usually urgent but concentration in a single industry, however good, or too big a stake in one company, poses an unnecessary risk. If you have this situation, try to work out of it in an orderly way. When you like a company or an industry very much the temptation to overdo it is very strong. It is something I have to fight all the time. Remember, diversification is your insurance policy.

There is one kind of concentration that requires special attention because it is so common and so dangerous. That is loading up on the stock of your employer. Many people who do this are not investors, in that they have no knowledge of, or interest in, the market. They are savers who have been offered an attractive savings plan and are loyal employees. Selling the company's stock would seem disloyal. But look at it this way, your salary and your pension, and your health benefits are all dependent on your company. Investing in the company also, is putting too many eggs in one basket. What I did was participate in the company's stock purchase plan. Then the day the stock certificates were delivered, I sold the stock. This did not hurt the company and it improved my security.

If you have Fixed Income Investments

Suppose you have little or no investments in stocks, but the bulk of your savings are in fixed rate investments like CDs, bonds, or the money market. From what we have seen of the comparative performance of long term investments, the odds overwhelmingly favor common stocks. If you are already retired, it requires different action that is covered in a later chapter. However, if you are still working, it is only prudent that, with all deliberate speed you switch your investments to carefully selected common stocks. BUT, a word of warning: you will be in a very different ball game, and you should be prepared for the new rules. There will be some volatility in the prices of your securities. The income, on the other hand, while lower, will be very stable and will grow every year. They will go up in the long run, but in the meantime they will fluctuate. If you are thoroughly convinced and confident that common stocks are the best investment and that the companies you have selected are sound, you can be cool and feel secure. But, while stocks go up two years out of three, the other year they stagnate or go down. The cool investor rides out the rough spots. Remember that when your stock goes down with the market you have not lost anything. Your company is just as sound as it was last week, or last month. You are still getting your regular dividends. If it is a sound company the only way you can lose is to sell. In the stock market panic is a loser. If you fear that volatility will make you nervous, you should stick to fixed income. The financial advantage of stocks, while great, does not compensate for the worry.

Starting From Scratch

If you have little or no savings, but want to create a fund for your retirement, it takes a different strategy to begin. While there are other ways to get started, I will describe two different approaches.

First, Direct Purchase

Many companies sell stock directly to their shareholders with little or no commission. This is most commonly done by voluntary automatic reinvestment of dividends. Most of these plans also permit the shareholder to contribute additional cash as well, usually specifying a minimum and a maximum contribution. The minimum is usually $10 or $25 per week, month, or quarter, depending on the plan. You will not have to worry about the maximums, because they are all in the thousands of dollars.

How to Use this Option

If I am just starting out and am not a shareholder, how does this apply to me? Most of these plans are accessible to ALL shareholders. This means that, even if you own only one share, registered in your own name, you can participate. If you think about it, this option has a great potential. Let us take an example of a start-up investor who has $1,000 saved up and wants to invest $50 a week. She wants a diversified portfolio from the start, but building a diversified portfolio and adding $50 per week through a broker would result in prohibitive costs. She can, however, buy one share of each of 10 companies that have dividend reinvestment plans. Suppose the average price is $40 per share and her minimum commission for each purchase is $30, her cost would be $700. The $300 commission would be a huge percentage, but it is like an initiation fee and there would be no commission or possibly a very small one on all future purchases. As soon as she buys these shares, not even waiting for the delivery of the stock certificate, she should write the company's Shareholder Relations Department and request an application for dividend reinvestment. She could rotate her investment contributions averaging the same amount for each company. Let's see how this would grow.

TABLE 21
Future Value of $50 per Week 12% Growth Rate

5 YEARS	$17,826
10 YEARS	50,286
15 YEARS	109,389

After 10 years, even if she never increased his contribution, which she probably would, she would have an average of $5,000 in each stock and would be in a position to invest through a broker if she wished. Incidentally, the company will regularly furnish you information about the status of your account as well as the necessary tax information.

How to Find these Companies

First try the reference section of your public library. Frequent articles on this subject are published. The American Association of Individual Investors recently published a list. If all else fails, make a list of companies you are interested in and write their Shareholder Relations Department requesting a copy of their dividend reinvestment plan.

You are not locked in

If it happens that after some time one of your companies begins to falter, you can sell your shares, usually through the plan itself and, using the proceeds from the sale, select another. This seems like a lot of work, and it is, but it not only saves you a lot of money, but it accomplishes something you couldn't otherwise do.

First, you have selected your own portfolio and are in full control of your investments. Second, you are not paying any management fee every year and little if any commissions, except for your initial purchase. Third, you are becoming more familiar with the way securities markets work and will be more comfortable with your investments.

The Second Method, the Mutual Fund

If you do not want to buy direct, for an investor starting from scratch, a mutual fund is the only practical alternative. The results will not be nearly as good, and it may get you in lazy habits, but it will save time although it will not prepare you for the time when you will want to start managing your own assets. If I had to start relying on a mutual fund the only type I would consider would be an S&P 500 Index Fund. They out perform 80% of the stock mutual funds and I like favorable odds like 4:1. You will need to check their requirements for initial investment and subsequent deposits, and check their other rules and regulations as well. It will pay dividends which you can plow back into the fund. You will find publications in your library that will tell you more about mutual funds than you'll ever want to know. Before you invest in any fund be sure you know all its rules.

No Load, No Transaction Fees?

This is the old free lunch gimmick. No matter what anyone tells you or how plausibly they explain, NOTHING is free. Transactions are being executed. The people who are doing the work are being paid, they are using office space, furniture, telephones, and computers, none of which are free. There is a fund manager and a staff. Somebody is paying for all of this. Guess who? The words "transaction fee" will not appear on your bill, but you will pay for it under another name. This is not to say that all funds charge the same, it just means you have to read further than the label to find out.

When to Switch

At some point you will, I hope, want to switch to a conventional brokerage account. It is more flexible and less burdensome than buying direct through the dividend reinvestment plans. It gives you more control and is less costly than mutual funds. The time for this change is a matter of individual judgment. I would think it would be when you have accumulated $25,000 or a bit more. Depending on contributions this would take about 3 to 8 years. You could stay on the direct purchase plan indefinitely, although it involves more work and record keeping. A disadvantage to the mutual fund alternative is that when you switch you will have to sell your shares. There may be capital gains, although in many funds you will be paying capital gains every year. This would not happen in the direct purchase, because you would already own the stocks you want and would just be removing the shares from company custody and either keeping the certificates yourself or depositing them with a broker. This would not trigger a capital gains tax.

Progress Comparison - Direct Purchase and Mutual Fund

Of course no computation or table can reflect accurately a real life situation. The following table gives a general idea of how your assets would grow with a fixed and very moderate contribution, depending whether the investments were self- managed or in a mutual fund. The difference between them is based on the fact that the average mutual stock fund's total return is about 2.7% below the S&P 500 Index.

TABLE 22
Fund Growth 12% With $50 per Week Contribution

	TOTAL CONTRIBUTIONS	ACCUMULATED ASSETS	
GROWTH RATE		SELF MANAGED 12%	MUTUAL FUND 9.3%
YEARS			
1	2,600	2,765	2,727
5	13,000	17,826	16,562
10	26,000	50,286	42,918
15	39,000	109,389	84,860
20	52,000	217,009	151,604
25	65,000	418,969	257,817
30	78,000	769,785	426,840

An objection might be raised that this comparison is unfair to mutual funds, because, even though the average fund may perform this way, I would not pick an average fund, I would pick one of the best. This is a very optimistic and unrealistic expectation. Remember that the investor who picked the very worst fund, and somebody did, thought it was one of the best. But suppose you succeed in getting one of the best, if you are smart enough to pick the best mutual funds, you are smart enough to pick the best stocks. If you do that your return will be greater than the S&P 500 and you won't be paying a management fee every year for the rest of your life. There is very little sense engaging in a venture against unfavorable odds. I think the comparison is fair and realistic.

This kind of table gives you a clue when to switch. But I must point out that by keeping the contribution at a fixed amount, the real value of your contribution is constantly decreased at the rate of inflation. If it were a percentage of the investor's income, the total would probably double or triple.

CHAPTER 15

Managing Your Portfolio

At the start your portfolio may consist of carefully selected well-diversified stocks. But there is activity in each and also in the economic environment. It is like a garden. It needs spraying, pruning, and weeding from time to time to keep it healthy.

Adding to your Portfolio

Your portfolio will never remain static. Your own regular contributions are of the utmost importance to insure a healthy asset growth. As these savings accumulate, you will add to your investments either by increasing diversification, if appropriate, or by adding to stocks you already hold. These additions can help you maintain a proper balance between different companies and different industry groups.

What Size Trade?

You will accumulate your contributions and probably your dividends as well, and when you have enough to make it practical, you will buy stock. Before discussing how much is enough, I would like to suggest one convenient repository for these savings waiting to be invested. Your broker is almost certain to provide a money market fund. If brokers hold your securities, they can routinely deposit your dividends to that account and you can send your contributions. Your money will be earning interest and it will be accessible to the broker to pay for your stock purchases. The amount to invest will depend somewhat on your broker's commission rate. For a discount broker, the amount might be $1,500, probably twice that if you use a full service broker. In any case, make sure you know the minimum commission, the total transaction fee and the percent commission you will pay. Of course if you reinvest dividends, you can add contributions in just about any amount. This, however, only adds to stocks you already own. If you want to diversify, you will probably use a broker. There is one thing to bear in mind when deciding when to invest. Your stock earns a lot more than the money market, so saving a few dollars on a commission might cost you in the end.

What to Buy?

If you have fewer than ten stocks it is a good idea to diversify into an industry that is not represented in your present holdings. But do not be so intent on diversification as to lower your standards. Do not select an industry just because it is different or because it seems "hot" at the moment. Although you may be starting out to target an industry, never forget that you are buying a company, and it still must pass the test of your criteria. There are some industries where not even one company will measure up to my standards, or probably yours either. Select 4 or 5 of the very best you can find and choose from that short list. If you already have ten or more companies, it might be a good idea to add to one of them. If there is one where your investment is less than your average, that is an opportunity to even things up.

Reinvestment of Dividends

You are already familiar with the dividend reinvestment option. Even if you were not on the plan originally, and even though you are now using a broker, reinvestment of dividends is a very good automatic supplement to your other savings. And of course it is also a good way to invest your regular contributions without a commission. Remember, for dividend reinvestment the stock must be registered in your name, not the broker's.

How to Review your Investments

You should list your investments with all the material facts about each one: number of shares, company name, date purchased, cost per share, and total cost, including commission and other costs. This is the basic information that does not change. Whenever you make your periodic checkup, which should be at least quarterly, you will also need the current statistics: current price, annual dividend per share, and annual earnings per share. With this information you can compute the yield, P/E, total gain, total annual income, and total return. The portfolio printouts show what these figures look like. Your review will tell you how your companies compare with each other and how you are progressing toward your goal. You can easily devise a form to use for this purpose.

A Computer Program

It is rather tedious doing all this manually. Worse than the inconvenience, however, is the fact that it may mean that you would not review your portfolio as frequently or as thoroughly as you would like. It would be nice if you could get your computer to do all the dog work quickly and accurately and print out a neat report. This can be done. There are many programs available commercially with a wide variety of features and prices. If you go for this option, it is worth taking your time and selecting one that will satisfy you. If you have access to an IBM compatible computer there is an alternative that can save you a little money.

Alternative Software

You have seen the portfolio printouts I use in some of the exhibits in this book. A program I wrote about 15 years ago produced them. They have been improved and modified several times. Its principle defect, from my point of view is that it keeps no record of the stocks I have sold. It shows only my current portfolio. Of course I keep a file of the printouts I make for my reviews. As explained in Appendix B, any purchaser of this book is welcome to use my program without charge. The program listing is found in Appendix C.

What to look For

One of the purposes of the review is to see whether your stocks are performing as you expected they would. The stock price is the most visible indicator, but it can be misleading especially in the short term. Volatility of the market can have a temporary effect on prices of companies that in sales and profits are doing as well as ever. If you have a question about one of your companies, test it against the standards you used when you bought it or your new standards if you have made a change. If it meets your standards, it is a keeper.

When to Sell

For a long term investor there is only one reason to sell. If a company's future earnings prospects are not up to your standards, or in the very unlikely event that its financial strength has deteriorated, it is a candidate for <u>possible</u> sale. I emphasize possible because selling is a step you should weigh carefully. Two factors will affect your decision. In the first place, you may well have a large capital gain and you may lose a big chunk of its value after taxes. Secondly, it will depend on the company's condition, whether it is just a little below your target for a short period and may recover, or whether it is on the skids. Investors must make this decision, and I can guarantee that they won't always be right. When in doubt, do not sell. BUT, when the evidence IS clear and you have lost confidence in the company, do not hesitate. The second worst error investors can make is to hold on to a loser in the hope that it will eventually get back to what it cost, so they will not have a loss. This process may take many years, or it may never happen. For example, it took IBM 9 years to lose ¾ of its value, slash its dividend and then climb back near its '87 high. No doubt there are some stubborn IBM shareholders who feel vindicated by its (almost) comeback, but they have paid a fearful price. There was a 5-year window of opportunity to sell IBM after the '87 crash to buy a better stock and recover the loss. A loser in your portfolio is like a tumor. Removal may be painful, but you'll be better off in the long run.

When NOT to sell

Now we come to the worst mistake an investor can make. There is a smart-aleck slogan often repeated by investors, "You can not go broke taking a profit!" Some investors have a formula to pick the time to sell such as, when its price has doubled. You have doubled your money, except for 2 way commissions and a capital gains tax. Even so, you have locked in a nice profit in case it goes back down. Sounds reasonable and perhaps for a speculator it may make sense. But long-term investments are likely to triple, quadruple, increase ten fold, or even much more. There are surely many thousands of similar examples, but I would like to relate one actual incident that I observed personally.

What Happens when you Do not Take a Profit

In 1934 my father bought 100 shares of American Home Products. It sold for $28 a share and paid a dividend of 20 cents <u>per</u> <u>month</u>, or $2.40 per year. This stock was not then, and never has been considered a high flyer, but its earnings and consequently its share price, have increased steadily for the past 60 years at about 11% per year. By the time my father died in 1974, it had split 108 for 1 and the new shares sold at $45. This meant that without reinvestment of dividends or any other contribution, the original stake had grown to more than $480,000. Each $28 share was then worth more than $4,800, an increase of more than 170 times. It makes these 10 baggers look sick. When should he have sold? Had he sold when it doubled, he would have made $2,800, and lost $480,000. Incidentally, by 1996 it had split another 4 for 1, and the stock price was $65. The price of the stock had increased 987 times and the dividend was more than 25 times the original price of the stock.

No Big Deal

At first glance this seems unbelievable, but when you look back at the chapter on compounding and at the Ibbotson study it seems more reasonable. Many companies, probably scores, have done better, but this is one I have followed personally for 62 years. My slogan for the long term investor is, **No matter how much profit you have in it, NEVER sell a winner.**

CHAPTER 16

Mutual Funds - The Opium of the People

A Text from Karl Marx

If Karl Marx were alive today, he would have to retract his description of Religion as the Opium of the People. Today, surely it is the Mutual Fund that deserves that honor. Although their average performance is sub par and fees are out of all proportion to their costs, investors are relieved of responsibility of managing their affairs and making decisions. They live in a happy never-never land of low profits and an indestructible confidence that the fund manager's top priority is the customer's best interest.

Your Assets

Your investments will not manage themselves. Somebody will manage them. It should be YOU. It is not only your responsibility, but it is greatly to your financial advantage. More and more, however, investors are giving up all or part of this management function to hired managers. Except when the owner of the assets is a child or is unable to manage his or her own financial affairs, I strongly disapprove of outside management, which is predominantly mutual funds. I know I am swimming against the tide, but I have two compelling reasons. First, the cost is excessive, and secondly, only partly because of the cost, performance is poor. These matters will be discussed in detail as we go along.

The Choices

There are several kinds of asset managers and I will list them briefly. They look different but make no mistake, they all cost too much and deliver too little. Except under special conditions, which I will discuss later, a prudent investor will avoid them all. The most common is the **mutual fund** where managers accept investments. With many restrictions and regulations, managers invest the money they receive in a pool of assets. **Brokers** sell mutual funds sponsored by others and some that are operated by their own company. In addition they often offer another service called a Wrap Account. For a fee, typically 2 or 3% of the total value of the assets in your account, they will manage your funds, investing them as they see fit, with no commission charges. **Banks** of course have Trust Departments which will manage assets, generally trusts. These are often commingled in what amounts to an in-house mutual fund operated by the bank for this purpose. It is usually possible to have a trust individually managed for a higher fee. **Insurance Companies**, either directly or through subsidiaries, provide a variety of asset management services.

The Market

The demand for asset management service is enormous. While the performance of these providers is generally less than mediocre and the cost excessive, there are situations where the alternative is even less attractive. One such situation is when an heir or trust beneficiary is judged incompetent to manage finances. Another natural task is managing pension funds. The most inviting target of all is the individual investor. These markets are very lucrative and have attracted the existing financial powers and have spawned a new one, the mutual fund which has already dwarfed all its competitors.

Mutual Funds - Why are they Popular?

A mutual fund is an investment vehicle that creates a more or less diversified pool of assets, stocks, bonds, cash, or other, which all its investors own in common. They vary greatly in character, from stock growth funds to those specializing in small biotech companies or Chinese bonds. The idea is that an investor with limited funds or little investment experience can invest in a wide selection of stocks under expert management. There is another and perhaps more powerful appeal. Our pre-packaged mass production economy provides us with many conveniences, often at very reasonable cost. The frozen apple pie or lasagna is not as good as homemade and it costs more but it can be fairly good and it saves a lot of time and energy. To most people this seems analogous. Why strain your brain when you can hire the services of a real expert for a mere 3% per year. We will evaluate both the expertise and the cost later.

Mutual Funds - Their Objective

You already know from their very expensive TV ads. They are here to help YOU help yourself - its sort of a public service project.

This was a sweet dream, but it is morning now. Time to wake up. The entrepreneurs who start up mutual funds are unrelated to Mother Teresa. They are more like you and me. Their top priority is their own interest. Like us they want to make as much money as they can as quickly as possible. Nothing immoral about that, but we should realize that the interests of the fund and its investors are somewhat adversarial. The fees charged to investors are not necessarily related to either the cost or the value of the service. It depends solely on how much an inexperienced and unsophisticated investor can be persuaded to pay. The good news is that these creative entrepreneurs are making fat profits. The bad news - their investors make only a fraction as much.

Mutual Funds - Performance

The S&P 500 index shows the average performance of 500 diversified large companies. The index is neither good nor bad, it just shows how the market is moving. Most mutual funds use this index as a bench mark or aiming point. To beat this index, even by the slimmest margin or to equal it, is a mark of success for a fund. The majority of investors, too, consider it an accomplishment to "beat the street". As a disciple of excellence, I consider this performance mediocre. How do the funds do? Of the stock mutual funds, 80% fail to achieve even this modest goal and most of the others just barely make it. For fund investors the odds are 4:1 their results will be less than mediocre, and their chance for excellence is just about zero.

Mutual Funds - The Problem of Size

The size of these funds has a dramatic effect on their potential. If a portfolio has assets between $25,000 and $2,000,000, it should consist of 10 to 15 different stocks, the strongest and fastest growing that can be found. The fund manager has a much tougher problem. The fund may have several billions of dollars to invest. There is one fund that has over $50 billion in assets. The fund manager may have 1,000 to 1,500 different stocks. To invest that much money the manager has no choice but to invest a lot in the very largest companies, GM, Exxon, AT&T, GE, Sears, and many others. Many of these very large companies have run out of steam and are just limping along and are very poor long-term investments. Of the companies I listed only GE meets my standards. What this means is that, while fund managers are probably better stock pickers than you are, the average of their 1,000 stocks will not do anywhere near as well as the average of your 10 or 12. Any individual investor who seriously wants excellent results will easily beat a mutual fund.

Mutual Funds - More Convenient?

We all value convenience and short cuts that will save time. We are often willing to pay more for an inferior product (or sacrifice a little profit) in exchange for the benefits. That is as American as apple pie (frozen, of course). But we all have limits on how much inferiority we will tolerate, especially when planning for retirement. How much convenience can we expect? The way most people invest, mutual funds are likely to be less convenient. Investors usually buy several funds, often a dozen or more. They diversify with funds just as they would with stocks. Everything about a fund is more complicated than an individual stock. The investor generally winds up doing more work and paying through the nose for the privilege.

Mutual Finds - WYSIWYG?

Is it true that What You See Is What You Get? Not necessarily. The idea is that a fund's investments will match its name or its advertised description. In many cases this is far from true. This is not necessarily a case of deliberate deception, it just means that keeping investors fully informed may not be high on the manager's priority list. It is sort of a "daddy knows best" attitude. Fund managers are usually given considerable latitude in operation. In a recent case a very large fund, supposedly a diversified stock fund was suddenly more than 40% in high tech stocks, a couple of months later it was about 10%, this kind of restructuring required sales and purchases amounting to literally tens of billions of dollars. The manager eventually wound up with a profit but, after all the frantic trading, did not even match the S&P 500 which just sat there. The fund manager then put several billions into cash and bonds, betting the market would drop. It went up and the fund suffered a heavy loss. The uncertainties in even the best funds are much greater than in a high-grade stock.

Mutual Funds - The Imprudent Scramble

It is very important from a marketing standpoint for a fund, if possible, to avoid a decline in its published results, even if it were just for one quarter. To beef up prices managers sometimes take a chance and invest in securities that may have no similarity to the fund's stated objectives. In a recent example a fund described as a Treasury Bond fund, with the objective of providing maximum protection of capital, was sold to a number of municipalities as a safe place to "park" public funds. In spite of their objective and their representations they invested in the riskiest possible securities, derivatives, and the investors lost 20% of their money. The scariest part is that the fund sponsor insisted that its action was perfectly proper. Some funds would never do such a thing, but as long as this action depends only on management judgment, this is a serious risk.

Mutual Funds - Is there a Reliable Way to Pick a Winner?

The short answer is NO. Several magazines publish lists ranking mutual funds and the reader would tend to think that the funds with high rankings would be the best performers. While it is very easy to identify the funds that did well LAST year, there is only a very slight correlation between last years results and next years. With stocks the correlation is strong, but not with funds. To illustrate the nature of these rankings, William Baldwin, Executive Editor of Forbes Magazine, explained that their rating system is intended to identify a fund's "personality", not predict its performance. So, if you want an investment with a lovable personality, this may be the way to go.

Mutual Funds - How About an Index Fund?

While I am reluctant to say anything good about any strategy that keeps investors from managing their own money, it is only fair to mention one type of fund that avoids some of the most objectionable features of most of the mutual funds. An index fund is structured to replicate the component stock list of a market index, usually the S&P 500. The idea is that, if you can't beat the market, you can at least keep up with it. There are a couple of obvious disadvantages. You can never use your skill and good judgement to do better than average, although the index funds usually do better than other mutual funds. You also pay management fees, but, since there are no investment decisions to make and no research to do, the fee is very low. The advantages are that it is predictable and you are protected against loss except for the occasional and temporary market dips. If you are too busy or too lazy or too temperamental to manage your own assets, this is an alternative that will not get you into trouble.

Brokers - The Wrap Account

The brokers have a little different twist. In addition to their own in-house mutual funds they offer the Wrap Account, in which they manage the customer's portfolio, typically charging about 3% of the value of the assets every year and charge no commission on trades. This has an extra appeal to brokers beside its profitability. Their income does not depend as much on market activity. Revenues from commissions are like a roller coaster - boom or bust. With wrap accounts they flow in a steady stream. Brokers battle with other asset managers, especially the mutual funds, for market share. In one way it is an uphill struggle because the funds are so well entrenched, but brokers have one big advantage, personal contact with the customer. They are not as heavy handed as some of the TV peddlers, but, as you deal with them, never forget they, too, are salespeople and it is the fees you pay that put meat on their tables. Beneficial as the Wrap Account may be for the broker, like other types of asset management, it is costly for the customer.

Brokers - Sales Tactics

In dealing with brokers, agents, etc., the first thing you have to know is that they speak in a special, euphemistic jargon. They are not brokers or agents, and especially they are <u>never</u> salespeople, even though that is their principal occupation. They are financial advisers or financial planning consultants. They do not sell you anything. They offer you a list of "choices" or "options". These are all "opportunities". You are not a customer, but a client. They may use other terms between themselves, but they try to avoid the word "pigeon". Of course we all are subjected to sales pressure, and we all know that the buyer must beware. We nearly always see exaggeration and hype, and even a bit of deception is not uncommon. Merchandise is sold "at cost" or "50% off", which is usually clearly untrue. It is usually a variation of the "free lunch" gambit, something for nothing. Security dealers and asset managers have not ignored this tactic. The hottest pitch these days is for the no load funds. The name creating the false impression that the customer is not paying for the expense of buying the security.

Brokers - New Improved Label

There is a distinction between Load and No Load funds, but we are interested not in the verbiage but the bottom line and in that area it is a distinction without a difference. Studies indicate that no load funds perform no better than funds that admit they charge commissions. The No Load label is old and a little shopworn so they have introduced a new and improved version. They are now "no load, no transaction fee" funds. I hope you will understand that this new label, like the old is purely a sales pitch that is misleading at best. The only color of truth is that the loads and transaction fees are hidden and given different names. You are still paying for your lunch even if it may be called a cover charge or a donation. While the character of this old gimmick should be obvious to any adult, it is not. But most humans are naturally optimistic and **want** to believe favorable news. When marketers spend millions on ads on TV and other media to sell such happy news, there are millions of pigeons that will bite. I do not know how to apply it to TV, but it has been said that you should not teach children to read without also teaching them not to believe everything they read.

Brokers – What is that Familiar Aroma?

Like breakfast cereals, funds use well-known individuals to peddle their merchandise. Some, like one handsome young entrepreneur whom we see on our TV screen every day, are personality kids. Their transparent and convincing sincerity persuades the public to swallow their messages whole, although some of the more discriminating may detect the fragrance of "Eau de Balogne". One source of talent is the pool of well-known professionals who are retired. One of them advertising a mutual fund family talks down to investors like a preacher and warns them that they need professional help and where better to seek it than your friendly neighborhood mutual fund?

Brokers – Hidden Costs

In addition to the costs you expect, there are often costs you don't expect, costs you may never notice. These can apply to wrap accounts and several other kinds of asset management arrangements. The manager often holds substantial amounts of cash or cash equivalent and if this is all wrapped up in a single package with your other securities, you are paying 3% for the manager <u>to manage cash,</u> which may well be earning even less than 3%. This requires no skill or judgment, and the manager should not charge for it.

Insurance Companies

Whenever you need insurance, see an insurance agent. For an investment, insurance is usually inappropriate. But Insurance companies are financial giants and the growing volume and profitability of investment services has not escaped their attention. The first and easiest move was to put an investment spin on products they already sell, like annuities and life insurance. This led to abuses. Sometimes life insurance policies were misrepresented as investments. To cap it all the securities subsidiary of one of the oldest and most respected insurance companies was hit by a very messy scandal. Initiated and encouraged by management, their salespeople deliberately misrepresented some extremely risky securities and targeted as their market retirees and others investors who thought they were investing in the safest way possible. It will take many years and cost many hundreds of millions to wipe out this stain. The most disturbing aspect of all these abuses is the role played by management. An occasional "rogue" broker or agent is inevitable, but what can we think about management, and how can we protect ourselves?

Other Insurance Problems

One type of investment insurance companies have long featured is the annuity. This usually means a large investment up front and the company will pay an agreed sum periodically as long as you live. This is a very competitive market and some companies, seeking a competitive edge, invested their customers' funds in risky high-income securities such as junk bonds. As the recession developed and interest rates dropped, some of these bonds defaulted and some of the insurance companies defaulted on their annuities with heavy losses to individuals and pension funds. Recently a new feature has been offered, a variable annuity with payment varying with changes in interest rates. It is interesting to know that a salesman selling a variable annuity often gets a much higher commission than for selling the fixed rate variety. Can you guess why? Perhaps with the volatility of interest rates it is easier to increase profitability without attracting attention. After a while the customer may feel like the young Chinese student who was receiving an allowance from home. He got a money order in Chinese money and cashed it at the bank every month. He began to notice that each month the amount was a little less. When he complained the teller explained that this was not the bank's fault it was due to exchange rate fluctuation. Whenever he inquired, the problem was exchange rate fluctuation. After getting this explanation several times he stopped questioning it. One day, however, the drop was more than usual and the teller started to explain. The student interrupted, "Neva mind." He said, "I unnastand, fluct again."

Insurance - Forgive and Forget

It does not take long for the companies to forget these scandals, although forgetting is harder for the victims. While the investigations were still at their height and they were negotiating settlement with customers who had been defrauded, they were portraying themselves as the most trustworthy of investment advisers.

What does 3% Really Mean to Me?

Asset managers seem to be quite different, but they have one thing in common, a substantial fee. While the fees may not be identical, three percent per year is a typical charge. Three percent does not seem very burdensome, and by itself, perhaps it is not. But the addition of "per year" gives it a new dimension. That means 3% of the total value of your whole portfolio every year for the rest of your life, thirty or forty years, or more. This could be something big. As usual it will be prudent to figure it out. The following table gives us an idea.

TABLE 23
Future Value of Investing $75 per Week for 30 Years

Total Contribution $117,000

	ANNUAL RETURN	FUTURE VALUE	GAIN
Self managed	12.4%	$1,263,652.	$1,146,652.
Asset Manager	12.4%-3% = 9.4%	653,982.	536,982.

Some Difference!

This is a tremendous difference and you can judge what this difference would make to a retiree. Of course the self-manager would have to be an investor with common sense and a reasonable skill in evaluating stocks. Most investors would fail this test, but I am not addressing most investors. I am talking to YOU who would pass the test.

A Substantial Understatement

The above table understates the actual difference. I would expect you to achieve a total return, with dividends reinvested, of about 14% and the asset manager to equal the S&P 500, at 11.7. Suppose the manager's charge is a bit low, at 2.5%. How would that work out?

TABLE 24
Value of Investing $75 per Week for 30 Years

Total Contribution $117,000

	ANNUAL RETURN	FUTURE VALUE	GAIN
Self managed	14.0%	$1,724,277	1,607,277
Asset Manager	11.7%-2.5=9.2%	626,860	509,701

These of course are classroom exercises and are undisturbed by the volatility and uncertainties of real life. Nevertheless they are valid. A person might disagree with the values in the basic assumptions, although I think them reasonable. If so, substitute your own. It might make the difference smaller or larger, but the answer is the same - for any reasonably competent investor, hiring an asset manager is a loser.

Brokers & Managers - A Lion Rampant

We have seen how the cute little 3% pussycat eventually grows up into a raging lion. This is not an isolated incident. This flagrant excessive pricing is characteristic of the whole industry. By now they are accustomed to a pay scale where the peasants have an annual salary of $100,000, hundreds are paid more than a million, and top pay is 10, 15, or even 20 millions. To those in the industry this seems only fitting and proper. Considering their huge volume of business and the effect of mechanization, prices should be dropping sharply, but no, they are increasing. How do they establish prices? The following story makes it all clear. Several years ago, when interviewing a distiller, a reporter asked what was the difference between its low priced and his premium vodka. "Well," said the executive, "it is just a matter of pricing policy." In the same way the prices of these services are not related to cost, but are set as high as the pigeons will tolerate.

Aux Armes, Citoyens!

Why do investors put up with this? Why not revolt and storm Wall Street's Bastille?

1. Average investors have little familiarity with the market and wouldn't think of questioning the broker, who is an expert.

2. Average invstors have no idea of the process of executing an order and don't realize if they are charged $300 for $5 worth of work.

3. The investors are not too sharp at arithmetic, especially the long-term effects of compounding.

4. The investors are not helping. In fact, they are shooting themselves in the foot. Instead of embracing the discount broker as a friend, most investors are suspicious or think it less genteel to patronize them. They also buy the premium priced vodka.

5. In short there is no sign of a grass roots movement.

But - Time Wounds all Heels

Help is on the way, but its progress is slow. Usually over pricing cures itself. It gives competitors an opportunity to undercut you and steal market share while still making a profit. In this case, however, the profit margin is so huge that a cutthroat price war would cripple everybody, even ones that might increase market share. The big players disregard the small fry and compete with services and advertising. This can not last forever, but, especially to us old timers, it may seem like forever. Discount brokers are increasing slowly, but the semi-discounters are beginning to crowd the big full service brokers. Eventually the discounters and deep discounters will force lower and lower prices. It will be like the old jingle:

> The little flea has smaller fleas
>
> Upon his back to bite him,
>
> The smaller flea has smaller fleas,
>
> And so on, ad infinitum.

The Greedy Landlady

In spite of the pending, though remote, doom, the arrogance and insensitivity of these powerful organizations is undiminished. They are still raising prices and adding fees. But as you will see even the most downtrodden will eventually challenge an oppressor.

The Parable of the Greedy Landlady

There was once a landlady who kept a close watch on expenses. One day it seemed to her that her roomers were being wasteful of the toilet paper. She posted the following sign over the toilet:

PLEASE DO NOT USE MORE THAN 8 SHEETS

Next month she was pleased to find a noticeable saving in paper, so she changed the sign:

PLEASE DO NOT USE MORE THAN 6 SHEETS

This time the reduction was less but still gratifying. Predictably, once more she changed the sign:

PLEASE DO NOT USE MORE THAN 4 SHEETS

When she went to check this time there was a sign under hers:

"Say lady, what's par for this hole anyway?"

The Customer ... Always Wrong?

One point I have not emphasized enough, although I shall get back to it later, is the low quality of service rendered by financial institutions. Overcharging is always objectionable, but if the service is good that may be tolerable. Since the advice usually varies from mediocre to poor, that is intolerable. I have already mentioned the callous attitude of high officials in the brokerage industry toward their customers. This was illustrated by a recent incident. In addition to their Wrap Accounts, brokers are cashing in on the mutual fund bandwagon by establishing their own in-house funds. While their brokers can also sell outside funds, the one time sale commission does not compare to continuing management fees. Predictably brokers are pressed to sell the in-house product. This pressure can be very strong. Recently several brokers in the Tampa office of a prominent firm were first disciplined and finally forced out because they refused to sell a proprietary fund to certain clients when they felt it was "unsuitable". In this case the local brokers were trying to give honest service. Upper management had a different priority - Greed. What are pigeons for if not for plucking?

They Get a Lot of Help

The popularity of Mutual Funds is not only due to their own efforts, they get a lot of help from the gullibility and ignorance of many investors. I will just give one example in illustration. Some months ago financial reporters noted that Sir John Templeton had sold out his holdings in one of his own funds which specialized in growth companies in "emerging markets", a hot favorite these days. In response to questioning Sir John said that investors had bid up the price of the fund so high that he could buy the same amount of stock of the component companies on the open market for 30% less than the fund price. It is hard to blame this on the funds, but it highlights one more danger. Even with good growth it takes quite a while to break even if you pay 30% too much at the start.

It Is not All Bad

However much we may deplore the ignorance and folly of average investors, or what bad advice they are getting from their brokers, we must always look on the bright side. It is all this irrational investing by the masses that tilts the playing field in our favor.

Man or Mouse? A Personal Decision

There are strong financial reasons for you to take charge. No one is as interested in your welfare as you are. No one else can select investments that fit your individual situation as well as you can. You, and no one else, are responsible for your own success or failure. This is enough reason to do your best, but there is another reason, perhaps even more important. What kind of person do you want to be - decisive, competent, independent? There is no better training ground than this. You will have to make tough decisions involving thousands of dollars. Your decision will not always be right, but you have to keep it in perspective as I try to do. I may not always be right, but I am NEVER wrong. This sounds like a contradiction, but it is not. These decisions are not necessarily a question of right or wrong. Even if you use the best judgment, things may work out differently than you had planned. Anyway the decision was made and it's over with. You now look ahead. There is no use digging up a dead horse. Your decision was good, it just did not work out, although you may say to yourself, but never publicly, "I'll never do THAT again."

Handicapped?

There is a straightforward way to decide whether you need to hire a manager. If you are physically disabled, you may very well require the services of a nurse. As you recover you can function on your own. Consider the asset manager as a nurse. If you are mentally or emotionally disabled, hire a nurse, but I wish you a speedy and complete recovery.

CHAPTER 17

Investment Advice

Be Skeptical

No prudent investor will accept <u>any</u> advice at face value. Faith is not a useful attribute for an investor. Even advice from the most reliable source, advice that may be excellent for some investors, may not fit your needs. Only one person can protect you from bad advice. You have the knowledge and the tools to distinguish between good and bad advice. Use them! Rule one is that all advice and other information about investing must be treated with healthy skepticism. This applies regardless of the source, including any advice or information in this book. The final test is whether it makes sense to you. If you accept my judgment or advice without testing it against evidence and common sense, you are in deep trouble. It is not because my advice is bad but because I have failed to get across my most important message. You are the one responsible for your own success, and every decision should be your own and should be based on the best evidence you can find.

But it can not hurt to listen

While the advice you are likely to get will probably range from bad to useless, it is a good idea to keep an open mind. Unless the advice is obviously hopeless, you might want to check it out. There might be an occasional nugget in the gravel. A closed mind is almost as bad as gullibility.

Many Reasons for Giving Advice

It is vitally important to evaluate why any individual is giving the advice. An acquaintance might come up with a friendly tip. Probably it is sincere and you can judge it on its own merits. However, if it is unsolicited advice from someone who will earn a fee or commission, you should consider it a sales pitch and treat it accordingly. If the adviser is a salesperson you do not know, even listening to it is not only a waste of time, but possibly dangerous.

The Pitchmen

These are the TV advertisers and the salespeople who make unsolicited visits and telephone calls. You do not have to wonder what is on their minds. They are not going to all that trouble and expense to do you a favor. They want <u>you</u> to do <u>them</u> a favor. You can safely disregard ALL this advice. Especially dangerous are those who make personal contact. Although in the small minority this is a favorite tactic of swindlers, forgers, and confidence men. In some cases the securities they sell are fraudulent and completely worthless. But even when they are not frauds, they may be misrepresented or overpriced.

Newsletters

The publishers of these letters are also professionals and their advice is for sale. Although the writers are not licensed and there is no requirement that they know anything about the subject, or that their advice must be good, it is apt to be pretty expensive. Investors will pay a relatively high price because, as they reason, one successful trade recommended by this expert may easily pay for several years' subscription. But how good is the advice? Well, it is spotty to say the least. One very well known letter publisher made a good living for many years without ever once being right. One problem these advisers have is to avoid getting in a rut. Maybe the best advice should be the same for several weeks in a row, but that makes dull reading. Subscribers won't pay for that. This is not only financial news; it includes more than a dash of show biz.

Newspaper and Magazine feature writers

They have a similar problem. Writers who are employees must come up with feature stories whether there is any news or not. In a dry spell they may have to dream up some kind of nonsense like "The Advantages of Maintaining a Balanced Portfolio". This kind of entertainment filler misleads many readers who mistake it for serious advice. It must be a great day for advisers or asset managers when they get an article in Forbes or a similar publication. It does not matter very much to the writer or probably the magazine whether the advice is any good or not. An old issue of a business publication is as important as yesterday's newspaper.

Your Broker - Hat Number One

If you use full service brokers, this is a special case. Giving you investment advice is part of a broker's job. Investors have confidence in their brokers and to some extent you rely on their judgement. The problem is that they have several different functions and responsibilities. They wear three hats and it isn't always easy to tell which one they are wearing. Hat number one is the broker hat. As brokers they perform the basic and indispensable task of matching buyers and sellers and executing trades. Most do that job very well. This is service you need and it generates commissions for them and their firms.

Hat Number Two

Wearing the second hat, sales brokers become trusted investment advisers. They are usually pretty high-class citizens. They are well dressed, well educated, and well paid, fitting in well with the upper middle class (where their market is). They are civic minded and probably belong to service clubs. Does this mean that their advice is exempt from skepticism and testing? Absolutely not! They may be helpful and give you some good ideas, but their investment philosophy is probably different from yours and their interests are by no means identical to yours. Their recommendations require rigorous confirmation. In dealing with brokers' advice you should make sure that the action they propose is consistent with your own objectives. Their investment philosophy may be very different from yours.

Hat Number Three

There is another reason you should be cautious of advice from brokers. When they puts on their third hat they are salespeople. Like any other salespeople they have an inherent conflict of interest. There are surely many times when their advice, while earning a commission, is also good for you. But devoted as they may be to your interests, they share one characteristic with you, their most important objective is their own welfare. Brokers certainly want you to be successful and happy, but it is the commissions you pay that keep them afloat. At first glance the sales hat often looks a lot like hat number two, and you may not be sure whether this is friendly advice or a sales pitch in sheep's clothing. The main thing is that there is a fundamental conflict of interest, and you should always be aware of it.

Who Buys the Hats?

Who do you suppose pays for all these hats? You guessed it. You do. Commissions charged by full service brokers are high. It is unlikely your broker will mention commissions unless you ask directly, but, depending on what you are buying they may range from 2% or 3% for common stocks to as much as 12% or 15% for some limited partnerships, and that is up front, right off the top.

What? Four Hats?

I am afraid so. The broker is an employee of a large corporation that has many interests separate from service to retail customers. Some can actually be contrary to their customers' best interests. For example, a company that wishes to raise capital by issuing more of its stock engages the brokerage firm. The brokerage firm underwrites this issue. As underwriters, brokers are working for the issuing company, and their duty is to get the highest price possible, and if it should be overpriced, so much the better. It means more profit. But where will brokers sell this new stock? They may share it with other brokers, but their best market is their own customers. Their duty to the stock issuer conflicts with their responsibility to their retail customers. The more they get from the issuer, the more it costs their retail customers.

An Example

I know from personal experience that such offerings, which are profitable to the brokerage firm, can be bad news to the individual investor. As an example, shortly after I had retired in 1972, a broker called me. His firm was underwriting a new issue of stock for Detroit Edison. He said that, now I was retired, this would be an ideal investment because like most utilities it produced above average income and he could sell it to me at the market price with no commission. It is true that many shortsighted retirees love utilities and would want to take advantage of such an offer. I have no doubt the broker thought the deal would be advantageous for me. Nevertheless I declined. This offer sounds attractive, but let us see what it really meant. It was selling for $18 a share. Suppose I had bought 1,000 shares for $18,000 and held them, they would now, 24 years later, be worth $28,000. The average retiree might think that was a modest profit. The only problem is that while the dollar value was going up 55%, the dollar went down by about 75%. In real money I would have suffered a heavy loss. The salesperson was not thinking about this but I was and he should have been. At least there was a happy ending. The $18,000 I did not invest in Detroit Edison has now, as part of my portfolio, grown to more than $190,000. That is a good reason to be careful about expert advice.

How Reliable is the Advice?

You may run across brokers or advisers you trust completely to give you the best advice they know how. Even in such a case, how reliable is that advice? The broker who gave me the advice to buy Detroit Edison was an experienced and conscientious professional, giving what he considered was the best advice. But Daddy does not always know best and investors have different approaches to investment, different philosophies. Brokers deal with many people and inevitably people's ideas and preferences influence them. Your approach to investment, if you agree with me, will be foreign to most brokers, and it is questionable whether your broker will be able to adjust. Advice that would be appropriate for someone else could be very bad for you. Aside from the dubious quality of the advice, you will also be paying for it.

IBM Shareholders - A Love Story

The Glory Days

For more than thirty years IBM was king. It became the most successful, the richest, and the most powerful company in the world, eclipsing the former leaders, AT&T, GM, and Exxon. As computers became more and more important it dominated the market, holding three quarters of the business both domestic and world- wide. It became a symbol, a personification of success. I remember when it sold for 70 times earnings.

But a funny thing began to happen almost unnoticed. Apple, Commodore, and Tandy, and others began to develop and market simple, primitive machines called personal computers. IBM had the technical and marketing muscle to capture almost the whole industry. But they had neither the vision nor the will. They miscalculated badly. They thought the personal computer was just a toy or a fad, sort of an intellectual Hula-Hoop. Even when they began to realize there was money to be made from the PC, they greatly underestimated its potential and entered the field in a half-hearted way.

My first Computer

In 1977 I bought a TRS-80. It had 4K of RAM and no storage memory. For loading and down loading files it required a tape recorder and an audiotape cassette. No commercial programs were available. We had to write our own, and the instruction book included a series of lessons in BASIC, the simplest of the computer languages.

An uphill battle

Professionals were contemptuous of, and strangely hostile toward, PC's. In 1978 or 1979 I gave a talk to the Rotary Club in Marathon, Florida. I was urging the PC as an interesting and useful activity for retirees. When I finished a member of the club, who was a data processing manager, who handled a large volume of data for financial institutions, rose up. He peeled my hide, explaining scornfully that a PC was only a useless toy and could never do anything more complicated than balancing a checkbook or keeping a file of recipes. Unfortunately the S.O.B. soon died and I never had the opportunity to rub his nose in it. There were people as early as 1975 who foresaw the future in detail. No doubt there were some in IBM, but they were not in charge.

Lagging performance

My wife and I were both stockholders of IBM. I was disappointed and a little uneasy that their efforts on the PC were so half hearted. But at the time it did not affect the bottom line. I did not know it at the time but in 1980 IBM's strategy planners clearly saw the market shift away from main frames. At about the same time I noticed that earnings growth began to decline and become erratic. Any company can have a temporary problem. For a good company it is reasonable to give it time to get back on the track. But after 5 years of inconsistent results I was more concerned with its performance than its reputation. By June of 1986, I was convinced its problems were serious and their corrective action, if any, was ineffective. So, I sold it. Most investors seemed unconcerned until the crash of October 1987. At that time IBM fell like most other stocks. Unlike the rest of the market, IBM did not rebound. It just lay there, stagnant at about 120 for a couple of years. In the next couple of years it slipped to about 100 and by the fall of 1991 it began a steep slide. In the summer of 1992, investor confidence eroding, the downtrend accelerated. You would think that by now even IBM's most loyal supporters would begin to get the picture - but no. Strangely enough, many of the professionals, who should have recognized this problem years before, remained steadfast. They had forgotten a basic investment rule, they had fallen in love with a company.

Unrequited Love

This error is perfectly illustrated in Figure 16. This is an article published in the September 30, 1992 issue of Forbes Magazine. The author, an investment manager in Boston, examines two alternative interpretations of IBM's disastrous 25% drop in the previous 6 months. Was the weakness in IBM a "danger signal" for the market? After all IBM had been a market bellwether for many years. Or was this price drop unwarranted, making IBM stock a super bargain? He reached the happy and optimistic conclusion that it was a great buying opportunity. Take a look at Figure 17 *(page 138)*. In September of 1992, when this article was published, you can see what IBM had been doing for the previous 8 years. Can you think of another possible explanation for the declining stock price? Would it meet your standards for a stock to buy? The author, apparently blinded by love, overlooked another obvious alternative. Is the company in serious trouble and the stock's price decline fully justified? A more appropriate title would have been "Bellwether, Bargain, or Dog?"

Dawn Breaks

It became evident soon after publication that the choice he did not mention was the correct one. The bottom dropped out, the dividend was cut 80% and, while IBM was not about to go bankrupt, its future was uncertain at best. Although it was quite possible that IBM would again become profitable, as indeed it now has, the glory days are gone forever. Of course anyone has the privilege of being wrong once in a while, but in this case I believe both author and publisher abused the privilege. Anyone can make a mistake, but it is hard for me to picture an investment professional writing such a piece at that time, or for Forbes to publish it.

The Market Knew Better

It is interesting to consider that while so many experts were touting IBM the people whose money was involved, the investors, were less and less impressed. It took quite a long time, but as more and more got the message the decline in the stock's price accelerated. This is just an interesting incident to many of us, but many innocent bystanders got hurt badly. Surely some naive investors were influenced by this article to buy into a disaster.

Figure 16

IBM stock has managed to decline sharply in a rising market. But don't write the company off.

Bellwether?
Or bargain?

By Charles E. Babin, Managing Director of BRS Capitol Management Inc. an investment management firm in Boston

Is IBM a bellwether stock? Is the weakness in IBM a danger sign for the market? Over the last six months IBM's stock price has dropped nearly 25%. On the very day the Dow closed at an all-time high of 3055 (Aug. 28), the stock closed at $94.50 – less than 3 points above its 52 week low.

Fortunately, the case for IBM as a bellwether – literally a belled sheep that leads the flock – is unconvincing. To function as a bellwether, IBM's share price ought to demonstrate an ability to lead the market. Statistical testing fails to identify any such relationship. What's more, IBM's share price has moved in the opposite direction from the Dow 30% of the time on a quarterly basis since 1979. So despite its being one of 30 stocks in the Dow Jones industrial average, investors should draw no inferences on the market from IBM's recent drubbing.

A better explanation of IBM's weak market performance is in a recent FORBES interview, Aug. 10, with Peter F. Drucker, that keen student of American big business. Drucker said: "Big companies go through a rhythm. In the IBM growth curve, one pioneer emerged to dominate the field. When the company becomes mature, it has to fight the competition on every front – software, PCs, etc." In Drucker's view, adapting to today's saturated computer market means IBM "is going to be on the defense for ten years," much like General Electric in the Twenties and General Motors today.

This says to me that IBM is now a cyclical stock, not a

bellwether. With cyclical stocks "buy and hold" can prove costly. IBM is a case in point. At $95, the stock is selling at 1982 prices. But remember: Cyclical stocks are just that: cyclical. Bought at the right time and the right price, they can make you a lot of money. There's reason to believe no is just such an occasion.

IBM is not going bust. The dividend, which is probably safe, provides a current yield in excess of 5% - close to the yield of so-called growth utilities and competitive with today's money market rates.

And its basic business could be close to a turn because prospects for the economy are bright. There's a reliable, unbiased way to anticipate the inflection points in the economy, swings that are vital to cyclical issues, and you can anticipate these swings by monitoring three-month Treasury bill yields. In fact, since 1980 some 85% of the annual fluctuation in GNP was explained by credit market movements with a one-year lead-time.

As I discussed in my July 8 column, interest rates have dropped almost 30% over the last

Why IBM's a buy

IBM appreciation* more than	Probability of outcome
0 %	95 %
5	90
10	85
20	65

*By Dec. 31

IBM has become a cyclical stock. With the business cycle improving, IBM looks a likely prospect for a turnaround.

year and roughly 40% from their March 1989 peak (9.1%). This dramatically improved interest rate environment should have a big beneficial impact on the economy and, consequently, on the computer industry. If history is any guide, 1992's real GNP growth rate could exceed 4%, far better than the anemic economy envisioned by consensus thinkers (2.7%), and welcome news for an ailing IBM.

Interest rates can also play a role in estimating IBM's outlook directly. For June-December investment periods since 1970, some 40% of the fluctuation in IBM's stock price can be explained by interest rate movements. IBM, in short, is an interest-sensitive stock and is becoming more so. Measured from 1980, changes in interest rates capture about 75% of IBM's stock price variation.

The table lists possible appreciation outcomes for IBM over the balance of 1991 as cast from this interest rate minimodel. The bottom line is immediately apparent. Even with considering its yield support, IBM's prognosis is encouraging. At any price under $100, the odds favor a significant rebound for the stock over the next six months or so. A 20% move is not out of the realm of possibility.

IBM is looking good on a fundamental basis, too. According to David Korus, a securities analyst at Kidder, Peabody, the company is just beginning to ship the high end of its new-generation mainframe product. (Mainframes account for roughly one-half of IBM's revenues and proved to be its Achilles' heel during the current economic slump.) This, in combination with a better business climate and other product introductions, could produce earnings per share on the order of $9.50 in 1992 – up sharply from this year's estimate of $4.35.

For investors willing to buck prevailing sentiment, the reward could be substantial. Now is not the time to sour on the stock. Remember: no guts, no glory.

Figure 17

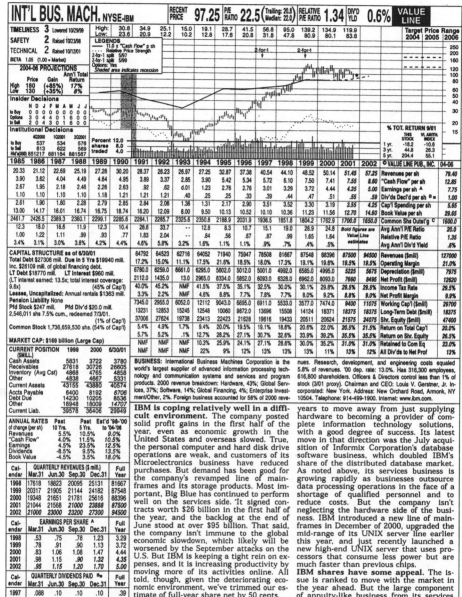

CHAPTER 18

Deferred Tax Plans

Great Expectations

Let us talk first about tax deferral. That has become a magic phrase like tax-free as it applies to municipal bonds. This device is universally praised and eagerly sought, but it may not always deliver as expected. It is like a hammer. When you need a hammer, nothing else will do, but when you need a screwdriver, a hammer is useless.

Some disappointments

Tax deferral is not tax exemption. You will eventually have to pay tax on your profits, and the tax rate may well be higher then than it is now. Even so, it can be a great benefit because, when the income is reinvested it is not reduced by income tax and it keeps earning and compounding for many years before it is taxed. So, what is the fly in the ointment? If you have an IRA, which is self administered, you are able to invest your funds sensibly and you have no management fees. It is all benefit. But suppose it is a tax-deferred plan that is under management. That amounts to a mutual fund. You pay a manager and have no influence on how your money is invested. Considering the performance of the average fund your results will likely be a little south of mediocre. You would almost surely be better off investing it yourself and paying the tax.

Tax Avoidance

Even investing on your own you can structure your portfolio to minimize taxes. Shareholders pay taxes on only the portion of a company's earnings that is paid out to them. Most companies retain a substantial amount to reinvest in the business nearly always increasing the value of the shares. This added value is never taxed until and unless the stock is sold. Some companies pay out only a very small percentage of earnings and some pay no dividends at all. If your portfolio consisted of companies like Microsoft, American International Group, Automatic Data Processing, McDonalds, etc., your taxes would be negligible, and with such strong companies you would be unlikely to sell and incur capital gains taxes. Furthermore, since there is no capital gains tax on inherited property, if you retain the stock for life there won't be a tax even then.

A Doubtful Benefit

The following table will give you an idea how it would work. I shall compare the results of an average mutual fund with an average portfolio and with a portfolio of stock paying 1% dividend. Here are the assumptions:

ASSUMPTIONS

(net return adjusted for tax)

Portfolio Type	GROSS Return	YIELD (Incl In Retn)	TAX	NET RETURN 31% of Yield Gross Minus Tax
TAX DEFERRED MUTUAL FUND	9.7	2.0	NONE	9.7
S&P AVERAGE	11.7	2.0	.6	11.1
LOW YIELD	14.0	1.0	.3	13.7

TABLE 25
Comparison of Tax Deferred Mutual Fund With Taxed Portfolios

PORTFOLIO TYPE	INITIAL AMT	10 YEARS	20 YEARS	30 YEARS
TAX DEFERRED MUTUAL FUND	10,000	25,239	63,699	160,768
S&P AVERAGE	"	28,651	82,088	235,192
LOW YIELD	"	36,108	130,379	470,776

Tax deferral in itself is good but if to get it you have to lose control of your investments and also pay a manager, it is difficult to justify.

Pensions

Most pension plans incorporate the deferred tax feature with the same advantages and disadvantages we see in other plans. Usually you won't have the privilege of managing your own investments within the plan, so you will have to put up with mediocre investment and a management charge. While the deferred tax will not fully compensate for these disadvantages, it does ease the pain somewhat. It goes without saying that, if you are allowed to choose your own stocks, by all means do so.

Contrary Advice

I am reluctant to mention this to a responsible and well organized person like you, but there may be a few readers who have not quite assimilated the MESSAGE yet. Under some circumstances there can be advantages to joining a managed plan instead of doing it yourself. I realize this is rank heresy, but perhaps as you read on you will forgive me.

It sometimes happens that people are forgetful or inattentive and, in managing their own savings plan do not always remember to make the deposit. Some may even let it lapse for months or years. Almost <u>any</u> kind of plan is better than that. There were many years when the U.S. Savings Bond was about the least profitable investment available, but if a person used a payroll deduction plan to buy these bonds for thirty years or so, he or she might wind up with a substantial nest egg. I hope none of my readers are driven to this extremity, but it is possible to do worse.

P.S.

One additional point. I believe there are people who enjoy bookkeeping and the challenge of complex calculations. I am not of that ilk. Nothing is simple these days, but I keep my investments as simple as possible. I already have enough problems that I can not avoid. I invest in a portfolio of 12 to 15 common stocks, well diversified, of the very best companies in the world - the strongest and most profitable. And if my portfolio is not the absolute best in the world, it's not for lack of trying. There is a question that bothers a lot of people. What about the GLOBAL MARKET? They advise that we should put a percentage of our portfolios in foreign stocks and bonds, in Europe, Asia, Latin America, and "emerging markets". Who is it that gives all this advice? It is the people who are selling specialized mutual funds and others who want to shake up the populace and sell advice. In my opinion this advice is not merely worthless but counter productive. U.S. companies figured out the value of foreign markets many years before these promoters did. Many are as well known in Beijing and Capetown as in New York or Chicago and some do more foreign business than domestic. You can do all of your diversification here at home.

CHAPTER 19

THE FREE LUNCH

The Bait

There used to be and perhaps there still is a marketing device used by saloons and barrooms, called a free lunch. Whether at a high toned place on Lexington Avenue or a waterfront saloon on Tenth Avenue, there were cold cuts and potato salad or salami, rye bread, and hard boiled eggs that customers could munch between their beers or their Martinis. This free lunch was very effective bait to lure and keep customers, and in its innumerable variations it is still alive and flourishing.

Gullibility and Greed

Intellectually we all know that no businessperson is giving away profit. The free lunch and its relatives, the loss leader, the 50% OFF sale, etc. are carefully calculated to appeal to our human weaknesses of greed and gullibility, hoping to bypass our intelligence. We are so elated by our shrewdness at getting a free hard- boiled egg that we celebrate by drinking beer all afternoon. This tactic is not restricted to saloons, supermarkets, and discount stores. It is used alike by conservative businesses, swindlers and confidence men. It is especially dangerous to investors because their life savings may be at risk. The enemy may be a con artist selling bogus securities, or it may be a trusted, presumably honest, brokerage firm advertising "no transaction fees". A flagrant example of this was the action of Prudential Securities which recently targeted risk averse clients and sold them risky partnerships representing them as profitable, no risk investments. I do not know where greed starts. At the least these investors were eager for profit, but were so ill informed and so gullible that they did not recognize the danger.

The Magic Words

There are a few words that have sales magic, words or phrases that stimulate our natural cupidity. Words like free, tax free, close-out, half off, fire sale, below cost, no load, and there are many others. For example, we have tax free bonds. Did you ever wonder why our friendly IRS, usually merciless in extracting every possible penny from our pockets, has suddenly become a fairy godmother? Once upon a time, it was decided that, instead of collecting taxes and returning it to state and local governments, it would be good to help them by allowing them to issue bonds exempt from federal taxation. These "municipal bonds" are often called tax-free bonds. In spite of the attractive name, the benefit often does not flow through to the investor. The issuers pay a lower interest rate than a taxable corporate bond, which just about wipes out the tax-advantage. No free lunch here. It all comes out in the wash. Despite their largely illusory advantage, the magic words do their work and they are highly prized by many investors. Tax free or not, bonds do not make the grade.

A Reality Check

The benefit of a tax free bond depends on an investor's tax rate and the yield he or she can get from ordinary taxable securities. There is a formula that will tell you at once which investment is the more profitable. If you divide the tax-free yield by 1 minus your tax rate, it will give you the equivalent total return of a taxable security. That sounds complicated, but I shall give an example. Suppose your tax rate is 31% (.31) and you are considering a 5% municipal bond. Divide the tax free yield, 5%, by 1 minus .31, or .69. That equals 7.25% for a taxable investment.. Since the total return on the average common stock is more than 10%, you would need nearly 7% tax free to match that.

I Fear the Greeks

Of course this device is not an ethnic characteristic just because the Greeks used it in the Trojan War. It is one way clever operators like Ulysses in the Trojan Horse Caper, take advantage of our greed and gullibility. I saw it used on TV today and the pitchman was no Greek. This "no transaction fee" or "disappearing cost" pitch reminds me of an incident many years ago. One of my colleagues submitted an expense voucher which included a cleaning bill. A waiter had spilled soup on his suit while he was on a business trip. His boss would not approve it, saying it might just as easily have happened had he been home. My friend rewrote the voucher without the offending item. As he finished he said to me, "He will not see any item for cleaning this time, but it will be there."

How to get a Bargain

Whatever you buy may well be worth less than you pay for it, but how can you get something that is worth more? In other words a bargain. The way to do that is to know more, being smarter, more decisive, or having better judgment than the seller. When a stock becomes a bargain, investors often don't react promptly. They think it over, sometimes for hours, sometimes days, sometimes months. If you find such a situation and have confidence in your own judgment, it is important to be decisive and act immediately. I'll give a couple of examples. When Philip Morris decided to buy Kraft, it looked like a sensible idea in its gradual move toward non-tobacco businesses. I saw the news in the morning paper which I got in the mail at about 1:30 PM, so I was a little late getting it. The stock had closed at $100 the previous day. This seemed bullish to me and I called my broker and placed an order, but by that time the stock had gone DOWN $6 a share.

This did not alarm me, and I bought it at $94. The sharp investors had made a quick calculation that Kraft did not earn as much on its invested capital as Philip Morris so would dilute earnings. They apparently did not consider the savings in merging Kraft with General Foods, which Philip Morris already owned. When they regained their senses the stock went back up to 100 and kept going.

An inexplicable drop in price

In another case I had ServiceMaster. It had been quite stable at $22 and one day it was down to $18. I checked to see if there were any unfavorable news items. There were none and, sensing a bargain, I bought it. In a few days it was back up to $22. I never did find out what caused this. It pays off to know your companies well. That will help you get bargains. But there is a proverb from ancient Rome that you should always heed, Caveat Emptor - let the buyer beware.

The Unrecognized Opportunity

If your knowledge and judgment is superior to those of the majority of investors, and it surely will be, you can often find a real bargain. Once again my familiarity with ServiceMaster provided me such an opportunity. This company has been in business for more than 50 years and has been consistently successful and profitable. It had the conventional corporate structure. I do not recall the date, but in about 1986 or 1987 it occurred to management that a tax saving could be achieved by changing to a limited partnership, since, unlike a corporation, a partnership pays no income tax. The shareholders approved and the change was made.

A Problem

This created an image problem, however. Most such partnerships are established by general partners who want to start a venture in oil exploration, real estate, or the like, but they do not have the money to do it. The partnership is a device for attracting investors and raising money. These are often very risky investments and have a low financial rating. Although the ServiceMaster partnership was created for an entirely different purpose, it was tarred with the same brush and investors were unenthusiastic. The editors of Value Line apparently did not know what to do. The company was doing well and the narrative was favorable, but it was one of those, ugh, limited partnerships and was automatically assigned the very low financial strength rating of C++ (it has since been raised one notch to B, still a very low rating). Look at Figure 18. I happened to look at it in February of 1990 and you can see what I saw. The price of the stock had not moved in seven years. I then looked at earnings and sales and found they had more than doubled. Sales and earnings were increasing at an average of 15% per year. Stock prices normally follow earnings. This anomaly required attention.

Action

I do not like to make exceptions to my own rules, but I thought that Value Line's financial rating was wrong. To check my judgment I looked at Standard & Poors' Stock Guide, which gave it their top rating of A+. It was clear that some day investors would notice this discrepancy and the price would be adjusted. On March 1,1990, I bought SVM at a split adjusted price of $9.76. I just got in in time as it started to move up on about November of 1990. On December 31, 1993 it sold for $27.375, a total return of more than 30% for that period. I would normally expect it to grow at about half that rate, which is still very good, but it was catching up for the years when it was overlooked. It has split 3:2 three times since I bought it and has almost quadrupled in value in 6 years. There are many opportunities I have missed because I did not recognize them, and I do not worry about that. This one was so obvious it was like a license to steal. Nothing is exactly free, but there are good buys if you keep your eyes open and have confidence in your own judgment.

Figure 18

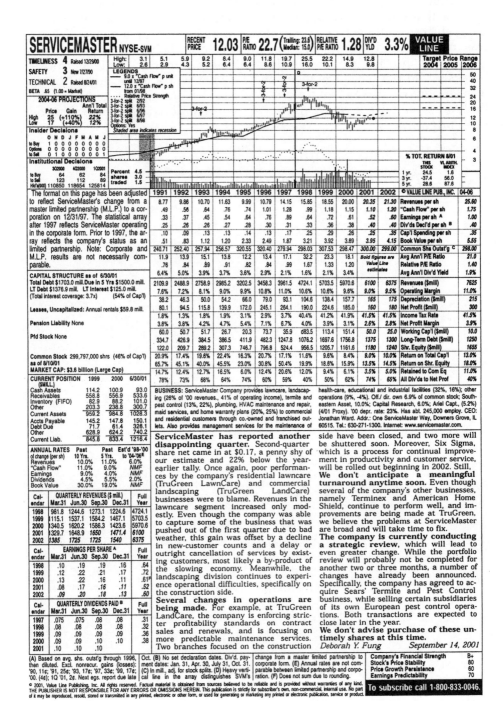

ServiceMaster has reported another disappointing quarter. Second-quarter share net came in at $0.17, a penny shy of our estimate and 22% below the year-earlier tally. Once again, poor performances by the company's residential lawncare (TruGreen LawnCare) and commercial landscaping (TruGreen LandCare) businesses were to blame. Revenues in the lawncare segment increased only modestly. Even though the company was able to capture some of the business that was pushed out of the first quarter due to bad weather, this gain was offset by a decline in new-customer counts and a delay or outright cancellation of services by existing customers, most likely a by-product of the slowing economy. Meanwhile, the landscaping division continues to experience operational difficulties, specifically on the construction side.

Several changes in operations are being made. For example, at TruGreen LandCare, the company is enforcing stricter profitability standards on contract sales and renewals, and is focusing on more predictable maintenance services. Two branches focused on the construction

side have been closed, and two more will be shuttered soon. Moreover, Six Sigma, which is a process for continual improvement in productivity and customer service, will be rolled out beginning in 2002. Still, We don't anticipate a meaningful turnaround anytime soon. Even though several of the company's other businesses, namely Terminex and American Home Shield, continue to perform well, and improvements are being made at TruGreen, we believe the problems at ServiceMaster are broad and will take time to fix. The company is currently conducting a strategic review, which will lead to even greater change. While the portfolio review will probably not be completed for another two or three months, a number of changes have already been announced. Specifically, the company has agreed to acquire Sears' Termite and Pest Control business, while selling certain subsidiaries of its own European pest control operations. Both transactions are expected to close later in the year. We don't advise purchase of these untimely shares at this time.

Deborah Y. Fung September 14, 2001

To subscribe call 1-800-833-0046.

CHAPTER 20

When You Retire

Plan Ahead for Change

When you retire you will face financial readjustment. This change can be rough or smooth, depending on your preparations. You will not be working for a living any longer. Your income will come directly or indirectly from your savings-probably social security, perhaps a pension, and a savings program such as I recommend. It is unlikely that your social security and your pension will be sufficient to provide a satisfactory living. The keystone of your retirement security is the savings account that you have personally managed. The importance of careful planning cannot be overemphasized. Every year of your working life you will get a slightly different, and clearer, understanding of the amount you will need and the amount you are likely to have and whether the numbers will match. It is always more pleasant to contemplate if you overestimate the income and underestimate the expense. But you can see what happens when you consider what this practice has done to the federal deficit. The consequences would be much worse for you because you can not print money.

Be Realistic

If you come out even, all is well, but if you will be short, there are two ways to go. Depending on how long before retirement, you can beef up your savings. If you still can not make it come out well, you must scale back your intended life style until it matches your income. This will be a very uncomfortable decision to make, but it does not compare to the problems you will face if you try to live beyond your means. If you overspend, every day gets you deeper in the hole. Since you have retired, there is no way out. If you face the facts, you can move to an apartment or to some other less expensive location. Do not stretch your budget, give yourself a little elbow room. Above all, do not wait until you are already retired to figure this out, being forced to make hard decisions under heavy financial pressure.

Portfolio Changes?

Virtually all professionals, advisers, brokers, and planners, will recommend that, as you approach retirement, and especially once you retire, you should shift the bulk of your investments from stocks to bonds. Unless your life expectancy is less than five years, this is about the worst possible advice. You are more likely to live 25 or 30 years, maybe longer. I have already been retired for more than 24 years and I expect to survive at least 10 or 15 years more. These advisers are giving advice by remote control. This is a classroom exercise. They all have one thing in common. They are not retired. They are giving us a road map to a place they have never been. Their solution is simple, straightforward, and 100% wrong. I have a better solution and I **have** been there. It is not as easy, there is no easy solution to a tough problem, but it will work.

Fifty Years Too Late

As a matter of fact the advisers are about fifty-five years late with this advice. In those days there was no tax on long term capital gains, life expectancy was shorter and people retired later, so they did not live as long in retirement. They could cash in their long term gains (six months or more) without the heavy tax penalty we have today. They did not have the energy or live long enough in which to use it. Today all these factors have changed.

If It Ain't Broke

Suppose as you got nearer to retirement, you left your portfolio unchanged and kept managing it as before. The only difference would be that when you were making a change for normal reasons, you would replace a high performance stock with a growth stock that grows a little slower and pays a higher dividend. Even if your initial retirement income is less than ideal, there is no reason to abandon the strategy that has worked so well and with which you are familiar. I strongly urge you not to change your investment policy. Your investment income will certainly increase substantially faster than inflation, and each year you will have a little more elbow room, and your capital will continue to grow. This will give you and your spouse the best protection against catastrophe and a bit more for your heirs, if that matters to you.

If You come up Short

If, instead, your income is less than you think necessary, you are in a tough spot. There is no magic wand. You are faced with two alternatives, both of them unattractive. You can hang on to your stocks and tighten your belt. This will mean lowering your standard of living. The other choice is to try increasing your income by moving into higher yielding investments. The first alternative is very difficult to accept, and the second, which may also involve a somewhat lesser lowering of your standard of living, is a trap. While the first choice will gradually ease as dividends increase faster than inflation, the second will shrink year by year. If you shift your stock you will have less to reinvest due to the capital gains tax and brokerage commissions. However you approach this situation, take your time in deciding. If you must go to a higher yield, there is the choice between bonds and electric utilities, oils, etc. While I usually advise avoiding utilities, they are preferable to bonds. While they barely keep up with inflation, you have a good chance for some growth in both income and capital. You would rather find a magic solution. There is none, but there are plenty of persuasive slight of hand artists who will try to convince you they have one. And remember they are not trying to do you a favor, they are trying to get their hands in your pocket. The solution will be hard to resist, but no matter how good it looks, investigate it CAREFULLY.

The Alternatives

Let us look at the alternatives and see how they match up. Suppose you have accumulated $250,000. If you retain the investments, you will still have the full amount and will continue to get the dividend income. Both dividends and capital will continue to grow at a rate of 8 to 10 percent per year. If you sell to buy higher yielding stocks or bonds, after taxes your assets will shrink, possibly by as much as 25%. This would leave you $187,500. You would get a higher yield, but no growth in either capital or income. Both would be eroded by inflation.

How Much Risk? How Long Will You Live?

Let us take a look at some options.

TABLE 26
Keep Present Stocks, Yield 2.5%, Growth 10 % Rate
(adjusted for 3.1% inflation)

TIME	VALUE OF PRINCIPAL	VALUE OF INCOME
START	250,000	6,250
5 YEARS	349,002	8,725
10 YEARS	4877210	12,160
15 YEARS	680,151	17,004
20 YEARS	949,498	23,737
30 YEARS	1,850,424	46,621

THIS TABLE AND THE NEXT TWO DO NOT SHOW THE ACTUAL DOLLAR AMOUNTS, WHICH WOULD BE CONSIDERABLY HIGHER. THE AMOUNTS SHOWN ARE ESTIMATES OF FUTURE VALUE IN TERMS OF TODAY'S DOLLARS;

The first 4 or 5 years are a little lean, but then it takes off. As your other problems tend to get more difficult, your improved financial position makes it easier.

Let us try Electric Utilities

But suppose you switch into income stocks, like electric utilities. They will grow at 3%, just about keeping up with inflation, but they will yield at most an average of 5.75%. Of course, in shifting from your growth stocks to income, between taxes and commissions you have lost 25% of your capital. We shall see how that works out.

TABLE 27

$187,500 STOCK FUND, YIELDING 5.75%, GROWING AT 3% PER YEAR
(adjusted for 3.1% inflation)

TIME	VALUE OF PRINCIPAL	VALUE OF INCOME
AT START	187,500	11,250
5 YEARS	186,564	10,727
10 years	185,633	10,674
15 YEARS	184,707	10,621
20 YEARS	183,785	10,568
30 YEARS	181,956	10,452

This is a difficult decision because the situation changes so drastically as time goes on. There is another point to consider beside the income. If you keep the growth stocks, you build a very large cushion for protection in an emergency.

How about Bonds

Suppose you decide to get the best current income regardless of future consequences. You sell out and invest the proceeds, less taxes and commissions, in long term treasuries at 7%.

TABLE 28

$187,500   7% TREASURY BONDS, YIELDING 7%
(adjusted for 3.1% inflation)

TIME	VALUE OF PRINCIPAL	VALUE OF INCOME
AT START	187,500	13,125
5 YEARS	160,184	11,213
10 YEARS	136,848	9,579
15 YEARS	116,912	8,183
20 YEARS	99,880	6,992
30 YEARS	72,898	5,103

No one who understands the consequences of this strategy could possibly select it, but every day hundreds of retirees choose this course. The principal reason for this irrational behavior is that bankers, brokers, etc. have from time immemorial, insisted that bonds are the safest and most conservative investment. While this was probably true once upon a time, although no one now alive has ever seen that time, brokers, bankers, advisors, etc. still push bonds for "conservative" investors. Aside from actual fraud, this is probably the worst possible advice.

Make Retirement Plans Well in Advance

You can figure out ahead of time pretty well what your income will be, and, if you do not think it will be enough, face it in advance while you have a chance to do something about it. If your retirement income is going to be significantly less, do not wait until retirement to break the news to your spouse. Talk it over and decide how to cope. I am sure you realize by now that looking for the highest yield can be very costly in the long run. If you estimate that your retirement-fund will not be large enough to supplement your other income satisfactorily with the expected yield of 3% or 3.5%, you either decide to sacrifice a little more now or scale down your expectations for your retirement.

If Possible Do not Change your Investment Strategy

If, for one reason or another you have not been able to accumulate a large enough stake to permit you to maintain your accustomed lifestyle, it is better to face the facts at the start and make plans to modify your standard of living. That is a hard decision to make. If you start living beyond your means it will reduce your capital assets that you have no way to replenish in retirement. Since this is something you can not work your way out of, it is important to keep your investments in securities that will not be eroded by inflation and will continue to grow. In that way you will not get in deeper trouble and your income will gradually improve. I want to repeat the warning not to live beyond your means. It is almost certain that you have all you are ever going to get, and if you start spending your capital or let it erode from inflation, **it is GONE.** There is only one person who can prevent this from happening, YOU.

P. S. a Tough Alternative

Short of going on welfare or asking help from your children there is another possibility that has nothing to do with investment. Many retirees, either from necessity or boredom seek part time, or even full time, jobs. Unless it is something you like or want to do, it is a sad chore. This is an extreme possibility if necessary.

CHAPTER 21

If You Are Already Retired

Fixed Income

For a retiree the bad news is Fixed Income Investment and, worst of all, there is no offsetting good news to balance the scale. Most of us, as we retire, find that our nest egg will not produce enough income to support the life style that we would like. The cause of the problem is two fold. In the first place, we tend to see things in black and white and try to solve a complex and difficult problem with an easy, straightforward solution that won't work. Second, we are almost certain to get very bad advice from those we should be able to rely on, our broker, banker, or adviser. Since their advice coincides with our own inclinations, a poor result is almost inevitable.

Problem #1 - Inexperience

There are some optimists who do not plan ahead, on the theory that it will somehow take care of itself. Most of us want to be prepared for retirement which will likely be one third of our lives. Even with the best preparation, it will probably be the hardest third. Suppose at age 30 you , a very far-sighted citizen, start a program to prepare for your retirement at 60. You figure that a supplemental income of $14,000 a year, in addition to your pension and Social Security, would put you on easy street. So you decide to contribute $60 a week, investing that plus the accumulating interest in bank CDs, at an estimated interest rate of 4.5%. When you retire you will take the $200,000 proceeds and buy long term Treasury bonds at 7%, which will provide the $14,000 you planned for. Your future is now secure and, as long as you make your regular contributions, this problem is solved and you can forget about it.

Problem #2 - Bad Advice

Most investors want to be conservative. They have a fear that stocks are inherently risky and that, somehow, they might lose their whole investment. The bad advice you will get is prefaced by an explanation that is reassuring and sensible. You should be conservative and minimize risk. I agree with the sentiment 100%, but I believe the misuse by advisers of the words "conservative" and "risk" makes their advice worse than useless. Their brand of conservatism is described in the Bible in the Parable of the

Talents. A capitalist entrusted to a subordinate, a sum of money to manage in his absence. This manager was conservative, he buried the money until the boss returned. This conservative management style earned the manager a harsh rebuke and dismissal. Their use of the word risk is also misleading. Timid investors, especially retirees, think of the loss of all their savings. When considering investment grade stocks, the risk the broker or banker is visualizing is not business failure, but a temporary market dip, a brief paper loss, which soon heals itself, but may make the investor nervous. The real risk is inflation, an unrecoverable loss that compounds year by year and eventually devours most of your savings. This is the risk that is overlooked by both salesmen and customers.

If the Two Problems are not Solved

If you disregard changing conditions and carry out your plan unchanged, you are in deep trouble. First you find out that your company has discontinued furnishing health insurance to retirees and your Social Security payment will be 15% less than you had expected. The biggest blow is the value of your bond interest. It is $14,000 just as you had planned. What you had not planned was that your new dollar was worth only 38¢ of the dollar used in your calculations. In those terms it is worth only $5,320. If you keep the bonds for 30 more years, the rest of your life, the dollar will be worth 15¢ and the bond interest will be worth $2,100. You would surely realize at some point what was happening. It is clear, however, that time is a crucial factor. In carrying out our retirement program, it is vital to monitor it regularly and to adjust to changing conditions promptly.

The Trap

Suppose that, for whatever reason, you find yourself retired with a fixed income which either threatens to pinch or is already pinching. You must recognize that the source of your problem is the failure of your income to keep up with inflation. The principal offenders are bonds, CDs, money market funds, and other fixed income securities. There are also some stocks, especially utilities and stocks that pay high dividends that do not keep up with inflation. I wish there were a gentler way to say it, but unless your life expectancy is less than 6 years or so, you need to restructure your investments, getting rid of ALL fixed income and very slow growing securities. This is a difficult task - almost, but not quite, impossible. Most people can't face this ordeal, but failure to cope with the problem means slow strangulation.

A Rude Awakening

It is bitter to realize that, after 40 years of hard work, conscientious saving, and a comfortable middle class life style, you are now actually poor. Hindsight will suggest how it could have been avoided, but there is no profit in dwelling on that. There is no time for it either. The sooner you take action, the better. If your income falls short by 10%, a natural response would be to cut expenses by 10%, but then in 2 years you would be back at square one and this time it would be harder to fix. A better solution is to make a much deeper cut and start switching your investments to high quality stocks.

A Gradual Transition

Rather than switch all your assets at once, it might be less painful to stretch it out over several years. That way you sell perhaps 20% of your bonds each year. You would not get well quite as soon, but it might be an easier adjustment.

What about Stock Selection?

Does a retiree have different objectives and different standards for stock selection than a person saving for retirement? Yes, somewhat different, although many of the principles are the same.

Objectives in Retirement

1. Since retirees are using the income from their savings to supplement their Social Security and pensions, if any, they must obtain the maximum yield <u>consistent with safety</u>.

2. As part of insuring safety, retirees must make certain that their capital and their income will both grow at a rate higher than inflation. To remind you why this is so important, I will reprint here a table from the chapter on inflation.

TABLE 29

Effect of 3.1% Inflation on the Purchasing Power of a 7% Treasury Bond (Principal & Income)

TIME	VALUE OF PRINCIPAL	VALUE OF INCOME
AT START	200,000	14,000
5 YEARS	170,863	11,960
10 YEARS	145,971	10,218
15 YEARS	124,706	8,729
20 YEARS	106,538	7,458
30 YEARS	77,758	5,443

The performance in the first 5 years may be acceptable, but the loss of almost ¾ of its value after 30 years, when need is apt to be greatest, is <u>intolerable</u>. It is a regrettable necessity to invest in equities that will, at first, yield a lower income. It is hard to endure the first few years, but it pays off in the end.

Standards for the Retiree

With somewhat different objectives, you need somewhat different standards, usually just a change of emphasis. (refer to the **Value Line**)

1. The graph of price performance must show an upward trend and a relatively smooth and consistent curve.

2. The financial strength rating must be at least A, preferably A+ or A++. In view of the importance of income to a retiree, an A rating can be justified if the other standards are met. As always, if the financial rating

seems inconsistent with the other statistics and the narrative, it is prudent to check the rating shown in the S&P Stock Guide.

3. When we check the box labeled ANNUAL RATES, the annual rate of sales must be increasing. I do not put a precise limit on it but I like to see at least 3 or 4%.

4. The annual rate of increase for earnings should be 7% or 8% or better for the past 10 years, the past 5 years, and the estimate for the next 3 to 5 years. If one of those figures were 6% and the rest of the tests met the standard, I would leave it on the list for consideration. Note that sales rates of growth are often lower than earnings growth.

5. The annual dividend increase should match the earnings increase. Any significant difference, lower or <u>higher</u> is undesirable. A higher rate can not be maintained and is likely to move the stock price up, making it more costly than it should be.

6. A retiree should be cautious about a P/E more than one or two percentage points above average. A high P/E is usually accompanied by a low yield.

7. The yield ought to be in the general range of 2.5% to 3.5%. They do not all have to be the same, but they might average out about 3%. It is an almost irresistible temptation to look for the highest possible yields. Make sure, however, that you do not put yield ahead of safety or earnings growth. It is unusual to find a stock yielding as much as 5% that also meets reasonable standards.

8. The last step is the most important. Read the description of the company's business and the narrative. This part is quite subjective. Is this a company you would be comfortable owning? Have you enough confidence in its future that you could tolerate a crash like October 1987 without flinching? Maybe that is too much to ask. It is OK to flinch a little as long as you do not panic and sell out at the bottom as many inexperienced or nervous investors do. In fact if you have any loose cash, it is bargain time. A cool confidence is an essential attitude for a successful investor.

Step by Step for the Retiree

Some of the steps are identical to those for other investors, but I will point out the differences. Now let's take another look at Walgreen, Figure 4 page 75, and go through the steps as if we were considering buying it.

1. The first thing to look at is the graph at the top of the page showing the price performance of the shares for the past 12 years. Price performance has been very good. Value of the shares has increased more than five fold in the last 12 years.

2. Next, go to the lower right corner to check the financial strength. Its A+ rating is satisfactory if it meets the other standards.

3. Now go to the middle of the left edge of the page, to the box labeled ANNUAL RATES. 13% growth in sales is a good indicator of business growth. I consider this an excellent trend.

4. In the same box we find earnings growth, arguably the most important

of all our measurements. This figure, too, in the 13 to 13.5% range, is remarkably good.

5. The dividend growth tracks closely with earnings growth, and at more than 10% a year is highly-satisfactory.

6. The P/E, at 23.1 is substantially higher than the average, 16. Considering the steady growth in earnings it is satisfactory.

7. So far, this stock has passed all our tests with flying colors. With a very high growth rate combined with a good yield, it seems an ideal holding for a retirement portfolio.

8. Now for the acid test, the last step in our evaluation process. I see the narrative as confirming the favorable impression given by the statistics.

A Tough Job

Retirees who need to restructure their portfolios face a difficult task. No two situations will be the same, and I have only been able to make general suggestions. Like everything else in the book, these are only guidelines and, even if they can be helpful, they will have to be adapted to your own situation. While I have strong convictions about the general course to take, I regret to say that I am not optimistic that many retirees will be willing to take that road. In my years as an investment adviser, I have found little enthusiasm for strong medicine. In spite of my doubts of its acceptance, however, I must give my best advice, and I take heart in the hope that <u>you</u> may be the exception.

The Worst Mistake

Whatever else you do do not make the most common and most deadly error. It is so natural that it is almost inevitable. People will overestimate their income and underestimate expenses. This <u>never</u> works, and it can put you in a deep hole.

Advice to Avoid

There is a Siren Song you should avoid like the plague. Some advisers suggest that a retiree can live more comfortably if he or she spends a bit of capital every year. This is a very slippery slope indeed. In addition to the very real danger of outliving one's savings and finding oneself destitute, it is certain that the retiree will deplete the cushion of asset that might be needed in an emergency. No matter how you slice it, spending capital is an act of DESPERATION.

CHAPTER 22

What Next?

Now that you have graduated you are entitled to a Baccalaureate Sermon. What have you accomplished and what difference will it make to your future?

Uncertainty

Like any other graduate you are now stepping into the real world, which will be a little different from the well ordered academic environment of a textbook. It won't be completely strange to you but a live performance is different from a narrative of past events or a structured example. In an illustrative problem in a book you can be certain how it will come out. In the market place, using your own money, no matter how carefully you have planned, there is always an element of uncertainty. The process you have studied, including portfolio diversification, minimizes the uncertainty factor and will, if you follow it rigorously, make you more comfortable with it. As you gain experience you will realize that uncertainty is inherent in business, as in all other human affairs.

Figure the Odds

One thing I hope I have communicated is that the best we can do is manage our affairs so good things are more likely to happen to us than bad. The more we know about why things happen, the better we can plan for a favorable outcome. Because we wish our investments in the stock market to be successful among other things, we have reviewed price trends at the New York Stock Exchange for the past 200 years and the more recent studies of Ibbotson and T. Rowe Price. In addition I have made various studies for the book. The information we have available, if used intelligently, can be managed so as to be very favorable to us. We can imagine other events that are unpredictable or uncontrollable. They might affect our investments. Since these are things for which we can not prepare, they are best ignored. It is more profitable to devote our energies to things we can understand and influence. We must play by the present rules. You will not win every bet but, by keeping the odds on your side, you will win the game. Franklin P. Adams once said, "The race is not always to the swift, nor the battle to the strong, but that is the way to bet."

Go with the Flow

At the start of this book I gave a lot of attention to the forces that affect our investment environment. If nothing ever changed you would not need to understand these forces, you would only need a set of rules. Do not misunderstand me, rules are important and my whole investment theory makes use of them, but they are <u>your</u> rules. They are not arbitrary but are based on common sense and informed judgment, and they can be modified as conditions change. We are always more comfortable with the old ways, with familiar things. There is always resistance to change even when it is long overdue. Why do you suppose stock prices are always quoted in multiples of 12 1/2 cents instead of the simpler and easier decimal fractions? When the New York Stock Exchange was established, the U.S. Continental Currency was so unstable that businessmen used the reliable Spanish dollars, "pieces of eight," which were divided into eight reales or, in English, eight "bits". This is why a quarter is still sometimes called two bits after 200 years.

Tradition and sentiment are powerful forces, but Canada has made the change from "bits" to decimals and investors are enthusiastic about it. Is this just a matter of national pride, decimal stock prices to go with Celsius instead of Fahrenheit and kilometers in place of furlongs? Well, possibly not. In stock price quotations the difference between 'bid' and 'asked' prices, the 'spread', is profit to the broker and can hardly be less than 12½¢ per share. In Canada spreads have shrunk with savings to the investor and reduced revenues to the brokers. U.S. investors are hot to break with tradition but brokers are more sentimental and think the proposal needs a lot more study. Change is not necessarily bad, it may offer an opportunity. We have seen one example where failure to change has been most destructive. There is no justification for the very widespread custom of long term investments in bonds. It was good enough for Grandpa - is it still good enough for us?

Keep Cool

You now know more about investing and the forces that move the market than about 99% of the individual investors. You can venture into the investment world with confidence, an independent investor well qualified to manage your own affairs. But you need one thing that you can not learn from a book - PATIENCE. Although you understand what makes things go, in the real world, things never seem to go smoothly or predictably, especially in the short term. As long as you have made businesslike decisions stay cool. It sometimes takes longer than you expect for things to work out.

Still Plenty to Learn

Is this the end of your education? I hope not. As you gain experience you will probably find it interesting enough that you will want to learn more and polish your skills. I would advise against a cram course. Expand your knowledge gradually. How? You can look over your reference material and see what looks interesting or significant. One caution is don't latch on to some individual factor and assign it a higher priority than it deserves. We all have our favorites. One of mine is the long term debt. I love to see a company with none, but debt can be a useful and responsible management tool. One example, a company might want to borrow when there is an opportunity to buy a valuable asset at a favorable price.

Your Own Portfolio

Review of your own portfolio can be very informative. If you list your stocks as suggested in Appendix B or like the printout I use, you will be able to see very clearly how your stocks compare with each other and with the performance of the market as a whole. This will help to improve your future selections as well as to decide on changes if appropriate. Never look back. Do not rehash your past decisions and try to figure out where you would be had you decided differently.

> The Moving Finger writes;
>
> and, having writ, moves on:
>
> Nor all thy Piety nor Wit
>
> Shall lure it back to cancel half a Line,
>
> Nor all thy Tears wash out a Word of it.
>
> Omar Khayyam

The past is dead. The country where you will live and work - and prosper - is ahead. It is the future and that is where your attention should be focused.

Favorable Characteristics

Some years ago the David Babson Company's Staff Letters suggested that there were some general characteristics that were favorable to a company's success. I will not reproduce it verbatim, but here are some I can think of. You can doubtless add others:

- Ability to generate internally the funds necessary for expansion, improvements, etc.

- Flexibility in pricing. Prices for goods or services not restricted by stiff competition or regulation.

- Low capital investment.

- Low labor costs.

You can find successful companies that do not have these advantages. None of these advantages justifies relaxing your standards unless other factors are equal. Knowing these characteristics may help tilt the odds in your favor.

Now for the Plunge

The transition from the stable and logical environment of mathematical computations and statistics in the textbook to the rough and tumble of the stock market can be a bit unsettling. The stock market goes up 2 years out of 3, but one third of the time it is flat or down. These down years are not necessarily distributed evenly. There can be 2 or 3 in a row. If a new investor happens to have such a run of luck at the start it can be discouraging.

As long as your own companies continue to meet your investment standards, all you can do is keep calm and tough it out. Better yet you can buy more at bargain prices.

Individual Responsibility

It should be clear by now that it is not my objective to create a horde of clones or robots that will all follow my own investment pattern or philosophy. You are all individual investors, but more important you are all individuals with differing situations and objectives. You are in the driver's seat and if anything in this book helps you, so much the better.

Where did I Go Wrong?

No doubt I would be quite surprised at the strategies some of you will adopt. But I can take courage when I think of my long time friend and mentor, Brad Perry of David Babson Co. in Boston. I can picture him reading this book, slowly shaking his head and muttering, "Where did I go wrong?"

No Exceptions

You will make your own bed, and you are the one who will lie in it. I do hope for one thing, that whatever your investment style you will apply it with common sense AND CONSISTENCY. Adopt your own goals, set your own standards, but stick to them, make no exceptions. This does not mean that you should never change. It just means that you should not make exceptions. I am afraid that one time or another most of you will disregard this advice. You will say, "I know it is speculative, but this company has interesting possibilities. I think I shall take a flyer with $5,000. I might lose it, but I can afford that, but I might double or triple my money." The odds are not good enough. To make a profit large enough to make a real difference, you would have to risk too big a loss. But the greatest danger is that you might be lucky. It could easily become a costly habit.

A Dull Fellow

I am a pretty dull fellow as an investor. It is not an exciting approach, but I always think of the ancient Chinese curse, "May you live in interesting times." Whenever my investing seems to lack sparkle, I think of how interesting and thrilling it would have been had I kept IBM instead of selling it in 1986. As I said in the introduction, I am not trying to make you rich, I just do not want you to get poor.

A Poetic Thought

I want to end with a lovely poem written by a talented but unknown poet:

THE MEEK SHALL INHERIT THE EARTH

The butterfly has wings of silk.

The moth has wings of flame.

The bedbug has no wings at all,

But he gets there just the same!

I guess I am the bedbug of the investment world. I hope the old bedbug has been able to make some contribution to your future investment success.

Good hunting!

* * *

GLOSSARY

ADVISER An Investment Adviser is one registered with and licensed by the Securities and Exchange Commission to advise clients on the purchase and sale of securities.

APPRECIATION The increase in value of an asset in excess of its original cost.

ASSETS Property of any sort which you hold or invest.

ASSET MANAGER An individual or a company, such as a bank, brokerage firm, mutual fund, or insurance company employed to manage the investment of another's assets.

BOND An interest bearing certificate of debt issued by a borrower usually a corporation or an agency of government. They are variously designated as: corporate, Treasury, or municipal bonds depending on the issuer.

BROKER A member of a stock exchange firm who executes orders to buy and sell securities.

CAP An abbreviation for 'capitalization' used to describe companies, i.e. large cap or small cap companies.

COMMISSION An amount paid to a broker for execution of a transaction.

COMMODITY A basic product in trade, especially agricultural or mineral.

COMMON STOCKS A security representing ownership interest in a corporation. There are other classes of stock which carry special privileges or restrictions, or both, but the great majority are common stocks.

CORPORATE BOND A bond issued by a corporation.

DEBT a security evidencing a fixed amount of debt specifying the date payable and the rate of interest.

DIVIDEND That portion of the profit of a corporation that is distributed to the shareholders. It is usually in cash but sometimes in stock

DOW An abbreviation referring to the Dow Jones Averages, especially the Industrial average.

DOW-JONES INDUSTRIAL AVERAGE A stock index showing the relative price of the stocks of 30 industrial firms. It is widely used as an indicator of the level of the entire market.

EARNINGS The amount remaining of a company's revenues after the payment of all expenses. This is the same as profits.

EQUITY an investment representing an ownership interest in a company.

EXECUTE - EXECUTION The actual completion of a transaction.

GAIN (LOSS) The difference between the original cost of an asset and the proceeds of its sale or, if not sold its present value.

INVESTMENT Laying out money or property for the purpose of making a profit.

INVESTOR A person who makes an investment.

IPO An abbreviation for Initial Public Offering of a company's stock. It is usually a small new company, but sometimes it is a well established but privately owned. Purchase of IPOs is generally highly speculative.

LEVERAGE A device intended to increase the profitability of an investment. For example, an investor has enough cash to buy 50 shares of a stock that he believes will increase in value, so he borrows enough so he can buy 200 shares. If the stock goes up 25%, he has doubled his money. If it goes down 25% he loses it all. Whether it goes up, down, or sideways, he must pay interest on the amount borrowed.

LONG TERM INVESTMENT This is not a precise term but, as used in this book it means ten years or more, preferably twenty five or thirty years.

MUNI Abbreviation for municipal bond.

P/E The price of a stock divided by its annual earnings. This is called the Price-Earnings Ratio.

PURCHASING POWER The value of money measured by what it will buy.
S&P 500 An index of the prices of a group of stocks. It is composed of 400 industrial companies, 40 utilities, 40 financial companies, and 25 Transportation companies. I know it doesn't add up but please address questions to Standard & Poor.

STOCK EXCHANGE An organization providing a market for trading securities.

STREET NAME A stock registered in the name of a broker who is holding it for a client is said to be in "street name".

TAX FREE BOND A mythical creature. A name applied to municipal bonds which, being exempt from federal tax, have a compensating lower yield. The phrase "tax free" is a powerful marketing tool and is intended to convince naive investors that there really IS such a thing as a free lunch. And it works like magic.

TOTAL RETURN The total of the gain in value of an investment and the amount paid to the investor as interest or dividends. It is generally expressed as an annual percentage.

TRADER One who buys and sells for his or her own account for a short term profit.

TREASURY BOND issued by U S Treasury Department.

YIELD The amount of interest or dividends paid to an investor annually expressed as

APPENDIX A

We would also suggest that you refer to the current information sheets for Walgreen from Moody's Handbook and Standard & Poors Stock Guide. You can compare them to the Value Line page reproduced as in Figure 4. Moody's is somewhat similar to Value Line. The Stock Guide shows a condensed and abbreviated description on line 9 across the double page. By this abbreviation the Stock Guide lists many more companies than either of the others.

Each of these sources has distinctive features and, while they are in general agreement there are some matters of judgement where they disagree. When you have narrowed down a list of stocks for purchase, it might be helpful to check all three.

APPENDIX B

PORTFOLIO RECORDS

The first step is to prepare a form with a column for each item of statistical information you want to know about your stocks. Following is a typical example, although each investor will tailor it to suit his or her own preferences.

John Doe - personal portfolio _____ (date)

#SHARES	STOCK	DATE BOT	COST /SH	TOTAL COST	CURR PRICE	TOTAL VALUE	ANNUAL EARN DIV INCOME
SH				/			

The items in the first 5 columns will be the same as long as you own the stock. The figures in columns 6 & 7, share prices and total value will probably change a little every time you make a review. Column 8, earnings per share may change several times a year, while dividends and income will probably change once a year. To illustrate how this is used, I will give a couple of examples.

John Doe - personal portfolio _____ (date)

#SHARES	STOCK	DATE BOT	COST /SH	TOTAL COST	CURR PRICE	TOTAL VALUE	ANNUAL EARN DIV INCOME
SH				/			
200	AHP	1/22/81	14.70	2,940			
250	FOA	3/08/91	24.83	6,208			

This is the permanent information you will need for your periodic review. You will note the date is blank, because it will be filled in when you make a review. It will save a lot of posting if you make a few photocopies of this sheet to use as a starting point for future reviews. You will use this same form until you make a portfolio change. If you use a computer you will want to save this sheet, because it will be a lot easier to make changes than to do the whole sheet over.

When you make your review and post up to date figures it will look like this:

John Doe - personal portfolio _3/3/94_____ (date)

#SHARES	STOCK	DATE BOT	COST /SH	TOTAL COST	CURR PRICE	TOTAL VALUE	ANNUAL EARN	DIV	INCOME
SH									
200	AHP	1/22/81	14.70	2,940	64.75	12,950	5.18	2.92	584
250	FOA	3/08/91	24.83	6,208	39.25	9,813	4.18	1.60	400

You will probably think of additional figures you would like to see, such as P/E, yield, total gain, and total return. You can make up your own form with double the number of columns if you use condensed type.

There is also the alternative of using a computer generated portfolio report. If you have access to a computer, I would recommend such a program. If you are starting out and have only a couple of stocks you might not want to bother, but as time goes on you will need it, and you might as well start right. The easiest thing is to buy a commercial program, but, if you don't want to spend the money, or if you particularly like my portfolio printout, you are welcome to use it without charge.

The program listing and instructions for its use are to be found in Appendix C. It is written in BASIC for IBM compatible.

APPENDIX C

PORTFOLIO REPORT PROGRAM

On page 169 is Figure 21, a listing of the program for printing a portfolio report. For the program to operate correctly, it must be copied exactly. Each line tells the computer to do something, to take one of the many necessary steps, and each letter, digit, symbol and punctuation mark has a meaning and must be copied.

On 171 page, Figure 22, is the report generated by the sample program listing.

Following the two figures is a description of the program and instructions for its use.

Figure 21
PROGRAM INSTRUCTIONS

PURPOSE

The purpose of this report is to give investors a quick look at some of the most significant indicators in connection with their current portfolio.

It permits them to compare the performance of the various stocks they hold with each other and with the performance of the market index they choose.

FORMAT

It starts with a heading that identifies the portfolio, gives the date of the report and the market index for that day. Below that, in tabular form, it displays eighteen column headings, which identify the figures in the columns below. The report shows the following information separately for each stock:

1. Number of shares held

2. Company name.

3. Date acquired. If the same stock were purchased on more than one occasion, there would be a separate entry for each lot. It is very likely that one purchase of a stock would be more profitable than another of the same stock...

4. The closing value of a selected stock exchange index on the date the stock was acquired. You might select the DJIA, S&P 500, the NYSE index or whatever seems to you most appropriate. The example uses the NYSE.

5. Cost per share, including all commissions, fees, and expenses

6. Total cost

7. Current market price per share

8. Current total value

9. Current annual dividend per share

10. Current annual income - dividend times number of shares.

11. Current percent yield

12. Price earnings ratio

13. Present paper profit (or loss)

14. Months held

15. The percentage of your portfolio in this one lot.

16. The percent gain of this lot since purchase

17. The percent your chosen market index has gained (or lost) since you bought this lot. This figure compared to the previous column shows how you are doing compared to the market.

18. The last column shows total annual return, dividends plus appreciation. It is not precise since it uses current yield instead of figuring the yields for past years, however it is close enough for practical purposes. One caution, however, for the first few months you have held a lot it is very volatile and should be disregarded. For this reason it is programmed to print N/A in this column for lots held less than 6 months. As time goes on it becomes more and more useful. After a year it is significant. One more point. This figure is the _average_ total return for the whole time you have held the stock. If there has been a significant change in its performance, it will not immediately be evident.

At the bottom of the table is a grand total which shows the total amount invested, its current value, total annual income, the current yield, the total capital gain, and the percent gain of the entire portfolio.

Program Listing

This is shown in Figure 21 and its printout in Figure 22.

PREPARING YOUR MASTER DISK

1. Make an exact copy of the program listing as shown in Figure 20. The punctuation marks are just as important as the letters and figures.

2. Take a fresh formatted disk containing no stored files. Copy to this disk your program listing with the file name SAMPLE.BAS. Then copy to the same disk the COMMAND.COM file and the BASIC.EXE file from your DOS. NOTE: I will use a generic name "BASIC.EXE". Your version of BASIC may have a slightly different name. Use the spelling from your own DOS.

3. Now go into the C: drive of your hard disk and make a new directory, thus: Type MD STOCKS and ENTER -Then

Get into your new directory by typing CD\STOCKS

Put your prepared disk in drive A: and type COPY A:*.* and ENTER. You can now remove your source disk from A: and put it in a safe place for future use.

4. Now comes the task of replacing the SAMPLE data with your own portfolio.

Figure 22

2/28/92   Today's NYSE Index is 228.21

•Number Shares	Asset Name	Date Purch	NYSEa Purch	Cost/Share	Total cost	Curr Price	Curr Value	Curr Div	Total Income	Curr Yld	Curr P/E	Total Gain	Month Held	% Invest	Invest Gain	% NYSE Gain	Total NYSE Return
200	Amer H Produc	1/22/81	76	14.702	2940	79.000	15,800	2.60	520	3.3	19.0	12,860	133	14.5	437	199	20
150	Deluxe C	4/28/88	143	23.707	3,556	39.750	5,692	1.28	192	3.2	18.2	2,406	46	5.5	68	54	18
90	Equifax	1/6/92	230	15.641	1,408	17.000	1,530	0.52	47	3.1	17.2	122	2	1.4	9	-1	81
250	Fst Am B	3/8/91	204	24.830	6,208	30.875	7,719	1.28	320	4.1	9.2	1,511	12	7.1	24	12	29
200	Hanson	6/14/89	181	15.963	3,193	19.375	3,875	1.33	266	6.9	9.4	682	31	3.6	21	26	14
320	Heinz	1/24/85	103	10.477	3,353	39.250	12,560	1.08	346	2.8	17.1	9,207	85	11.5	275	122	23
30	Melville	1/6/92	230	44.867	1,346	50.750	1,523	1.44	43	2.8	15.3	176	2	1.4	13	-1	138
90	Merck	4/20/89	171	67.515	6,076	157.625	14,186	2.76	248	1.8	30.1	8,110	34	13	133	33	36
20	Merck	7/10/89	180	70.980	1,420	157.625	3,153	2.76	55	1.8	30.1	1,733	32	2.9	122	27	37
400	Philip Morr	10/18/88	157	23.750	9,500	76.750	30,700	2.10	840	2.7	16.2	21,200	40	28.2	223	45	44
300	SvcMastr	3/1/90	183	14.642	4,393	26.000	7,800	1.30	390	5	16.7	3,407	24	7.2	78	24	38
35	Stanhome	1/6/92	230	37.481	1,312	33.250	1,164	0.92	32	2.8	11.7	-148	2	1.1	-11	-1	-54
1,400	Bank	2/26/92	228	1.000	1,400	1.000	1,400	0.04	49	3.5	28.6	0	0	1.3	0	0	4
1,654	FIDO	2/26/92	228	1.000	1,654	1	1,654	0.05	75	4.5	22.2	0	0	1.5	0	0	5
Totals					47759		108,756		3,423	3.1		61,266		100	128		

Yield on the Basis of the original cost = 7.2%

PERSONALIZING YOUR PROGRAM

Clearing Out the Old Data

Before doing anything else you must display the program. While in the STOCK directory, type BASIC.EXE. You are then in BASIC, so type F3 (LOAD) SAMPLE. You can list a hard copy by typing LLIST and ENTER. The program is too long to fit on your screen, so you have to look at a section at a time, like LIST 1-200 or for a single line LIST 140.

I have reserved the lines from 1000-1999 for the data on stocks. All this data on the sample should be erased. Since the lines in use run from 1000 to 1110, that is what should be erased.

Entering the New

First you want to name the portfolio. This is shown on line 190. If you look at the title on the printout and then at line 190, you will see how it works and will be able to substitute your own label. That will only have to be done once. The second thing is to enter the date of the review and the market index for that date. Suppose today is July 14,1994 and you are about to post up to date prices for your stocks and the NYSE index. This information is displayed in line 210. You would type 210 B1=7:B2=14:B3=94:DJ=252.06 and ENTER. Obviously you will need to do this for each review.

Now for the Stocks

Although there are 18 columns in the printout, you need only 8 entries of data since some of the figures printed out are computed from the 8 entries. Following line 550 where the data lines were deleted, list this data for each of your assets:

1. Line number followed by a space. Start with line 1000 and it is the best practice to use every 10th line: 1010, 1020, etc. This permits interlineation if desired to preserve alphabetical order without having to change line numbers as you add stocks.

2. Type DATA followed by a space. For the rest of the line items of data are separated by commas and no spaces are used.

3. Number of shares,

4. Company name or stock symbol (limited to 8 letters).

5. Month acquired (example 11).

6. Day of month,

7. Year acquired.

8. Cost/share (total cost including commission/ number of shares)

9. Annual earnings/share.

10. Market closing price for the day.)

11. Current annual dividend.

12. Today's closing price (no punctuation.)

The completed line will look like this:

1000 DATA 100,ACME,11,10,94,42.214,2.63,260.83,1.00,45.375

The second stock will be listed the same way using line number 1010.

The computer must always be told how many data lines there are and this is done on lines 140 and 350. The first segment of each of these lines gives the number thus: FOR X=1 TO 14. In both the lines substitute the actual number of data lines in your program.

Saving the File

When you have modified the program and tested its accuracy by printing it out, you will want to save it for future use. To do this press F4, type the name of your portfolio and <ENTER>. The file will be saved under the name you have designated. Incidentally, the SAMPLE file will still remain in the directory. When you want to retrieve your file, press F3 type the file name and <ENTER>

TESTING

It would be surprising if anyone could copy such a program and make the modifications without a few errors. To check on accuracy type F2 to RUN the program. If it prints correctly, Congratulations! If there are syntax errors you will have to dig them out. One tip; sometimes the error is in the previous line.